THE
LAND
AND
PEOPLE
OF
ICELAND

Portraits of the Nations Series

THE LAND AND PEOPLE OF ARGENTINA
THE LAND AND PEOPLE OF AUSTRALIA
THE LAND AND PEOPLE OF AUSTRIA
THE LAND AND PEOPLE OF BELGIUM
THE LAND AND PEOPLE OF BRAZIL
THE LAND AND PEOPLE OF CANADA
THE LAND OF THE CHINESE PEOPLE
THE LAND AND PEOPLE OF EGYPT
THE LAND OF THE ENGLISH PEOPLE
THE LAND AND PEOPLE OF FINLAND
THE LAND AND PEOPLE OF FRANCE
THE LAND AND PEOPLE OF GERMANY
THE LAND AND PEOPLE OF GREECE
THE LAND AND PEOPLE OF ICELAND
THE LAND AND THE PEOPLE OF INDIA
THE LAND AND PEOPLE OF IRELAND
THE LAND AND PEOPLE OF ISRAEL
THE LAND OF THE ITALIAN PEOPLE
THE LAND AND PEOPLE OF JAPAN
THE LAND AND PEOPLE OF MEXICO
THE LAND AND PEOPLE OF THE PHILIPPINES
THE LAND OF THE POLISH PEOPLE
THE LAND AND PEOPLE OF PORTUGAL
THE LAND OF THE RUSSIAN PEOPLE
THE LAND AND PEOPLE OF SCOTLAND
THE LAND AND PEOPLE OF SOUTH AFRICA
THE LAND AND PEOPLE OF SPAIN
THE LAND AND PEOPLE OF SWEDEN
THE LAND AND PEOPLE OF SWITZERLAND
THE LAND AND PEOPLE OF TURKEY
THE LAND AND PEOPLE OF VENEZUELA
THE LAND OF WILLIAM OF ORANGE

THE
LAND AND PEOPLE
OF
ICELAND

By Erick Berry, pseud.

PORTRAITS OF THE NATIONS SERIES

J. B. Lippincott Company
Philadelphia & New York

COPYRIGHT © 1959 BY ERICK BERRY

PRINTED IN THE UNITED STATES OF AMERICA

LIBRARY OF CONGRESS CATALOG CARD NUMBER 59-12370

SECOND IMPRESSION

The author wishes to thank the Orlof Travel
Bureau of Reykjavik for their permission to
use the photographs reproduced in this book.

CONTENTS

CHAPTER   PAGE

1. LAND OF ICE AND FIRE 9

2. FROM PIRACY TO DEMOCRACY 18

3. FROM ISOLATION TO THE UNITED NATIONS . 30

4. THE GREENLAND MYSTERY 41

5. MOVE OVER, MR. COLUMBUS! 55

6. REYKJAVIK, SMOKING BAY 63

7. BLEAK NORTH COUNTRY 77

8. LAND WITHOUT TREES 87

9. MORE EARLY SETTLERS 96

10. SINGERS AND THEIR SONGS 105

11. FOLK AND FOLKWAYS 113

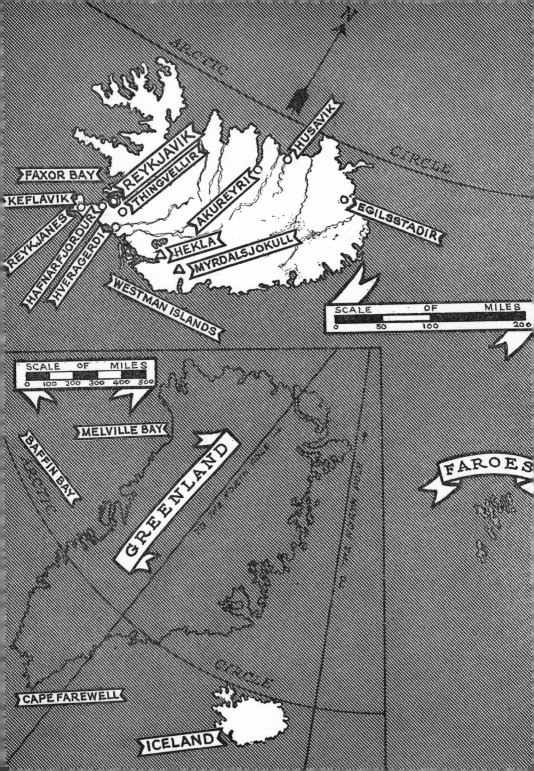

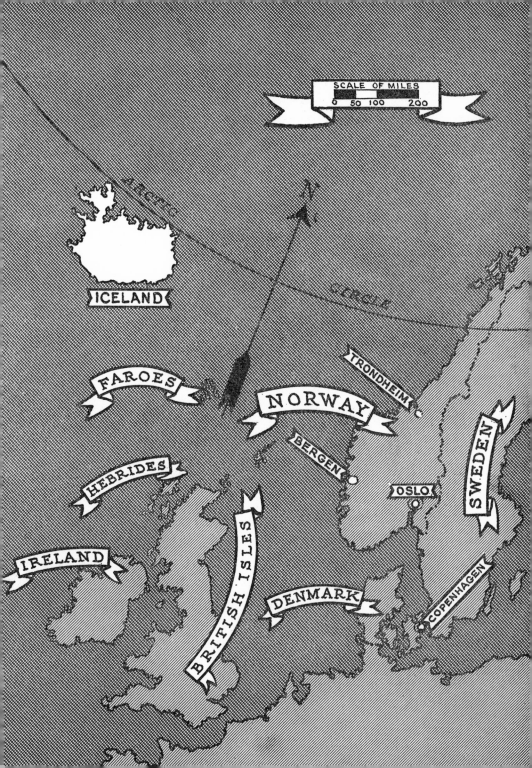

1

Land of Ice and Fire

Any mention of Iceland is sure to bring forth two queries. One is, how big is it; the other, how cold is it?

The first question is easy to answer. The island, just touching the Arctic Circle, and northwest of the British Isles only a short trip as the present planes fly, is 39,709 square miles, about the size of New York State, or Kentucky. Not a big island. And when you know that only about one fourth of it is inhabitable and that only about one fourteenth of it is fit for cultivation, it shrinks still further.

Beyond saying it isn't as cold as you might expect, it will take longer to answer that question about the temperature. To understand why, you'll have to know more about the background, which makes it possible to grow tropical fruit beside perennial glaciers. Iceland, like her inhabitants, has had a tough time of it from the very beginning. And this has left its mark to the present day.

There is her geological history, which is a short one as geology goes, for she is one of the youngest land masses in the world. She was heaved up out of the Atlantic Ocean not so many millions of years ago. In fact, she is still going through her teething troubles, with periodic fits of tempers and sulks, and now and then an hysterical volcanic outburst.

The last Ice Age almost obliterated her. The ice began to retreat from Iceland only some seven to nine thousand years ago, and the island's present geographical structure is a layer cake of her various stages of life and death. A bed of volcanic basalt and lava, sterile and useless, has slowly weathered till it can support life, then has been overwhelmed again by an annihilating flow of molten rock. This bare rock has again aged through the centuries till it could again support life. Again and again this has happened. In the Westman Islands, which lie in the rough seas off Iceland's southwest coast, about eighty of these layers can be counted, alternating strata of life, death; life, death.

At present, but no one knows for how long, the land is again weathering and growing more fertile. In the center of Iceland lies an icecap thousands of feet deep. Where this ice slowly melts and recedes it exposes a surface equally sterile; lava, volcanic ash and similar inert matter incredibly turned and twisted and tossed as though this black mass were a sea frozen in its most violent action. Further out beyond the reaches of the glaciers, lichens and moss cover the land; they look at first sight like a heavy layer of greenish-gray dust that has begun to blur the writhing black-brown surface. These lichens and mosses in turn—and the process may often be seen in a half hour's walk—live and die and produce enough humus to support small lavender flowering thyme, little white belled plants, cotton grass that blows in the wind with heads like so many hoary old men, and still further out, small stunted brush willow and birch struggling between hummocks of coarse bright green grass.

Iceland is a land of ice and fire, still a seething caldron of active volcanoes, of which there are some hundred and fifty on the island, and literally thousands of craters, large and small, down which between bouts of activity creep the eternal glaciers.

Of all of these volcanoes Hekla is the largest and most recently active, as well as the most famous. Her name means Hooded Mountain and refers to her cap of snow. During its dormant period Hekla's snowy cone points 5,108 feet into the air. The Icelanders take great pride in her. She has in the past done them enormous damage, but she is among their most spectacular attractions, even when asleep, and sightseers come from all over the island to picnic at her rough lava feet, to scramble joyously up her steep black sides and peer fearfully down into her crater. There are records of twenty-one eruptions; the last one, after a sleeping period of a hundred and two years, occurred as recently as 1947.

In the days of early Christianity in Iceland the preaching clergy used to compare Hekla's fiery crater, with its roaring current of boiling rock that poured from the bowels of the earth, to the gates of hell. Few medieval preachers in Europe could have had a more graphic picture of those devil-haunted portals and what the afterlife might hold for sinners.

In her recent outburst Hekla put on quite a circus. From a fissure three miles long great tongues of fire leaped hundreds of feet into the air, and a column of smoke rose 40,000 feet into the sky, twice as high as the mushroom cloud from the atom bomb. Hekla's loud rumblings could be heard three hundred miles out at sea, as rivers of melting ice rushed down the sides of the fiery crater. The ash swept across southern England and two days later reached Finland, and for thirteen months thereafter some ten square miles of un-inhabited land was flooded with the molten lava.

Hekla is the most recent and most spectacular of Iceland's exhibitionist volcanoes, but there are others that have in the past done far more damage. Volcanoes beneath the ice of the glaciers are an additional menace, for with their eruption not only flame and lava are hurled into the air, but millions of tons of ice melt into roaring torrents and inundate the plains beneath. Such a burst beneath a glacier occurred in 1783 in the western area of Vatnajokull; for a period of more than seven months and from more than a hundred craters twenty-two miles long, it flung out volcanic ash that was borne as far as Africa and Eastern Siberia. Seventy per cent of Iceland's livestock died in that eruption, drowned, burned to death or overwhelmed by poisonous gases, and twenty per cent of the population was killed or died later of starvation.

Iceland's early settlers could scarcely have chosen a worse spot in which to make their homes. As a pirate stronghold it might, in the beginning, have had its advantages, but as farmland on which a stable, productive civilization should be based it could not have compared with the land they left behind them.

Second only to the volcanoes in explosive drama is Iceland's Geysir, which means "to rush furiously" and for which all other geysers in the world are named. Seventy miles out from the main city of Reykjavik, on a rocky plateau which overlooks the beautiful valley, on a tilted rocky platform lies Great Geysir; a deep pool of clear water in a white silica basin all of fifty feet across.

This is another favorite excursion for the modern Icelander. They come on week-ends in busloads, a three- or four-hour trip over rocky roads from the city, and it is up to Geysir to perform. But unlike our Old Faithful, he does not perform exactly to schedule, in fact, between 1916 and 1935 Geysir put on no show at all. Now it is known that he can be induced to do his tricks. And with, of all things, the dose of a large quantity of soap. The soap, tossed into the basin, forms a covering over the surface of Geysir's hot water, shutting in the steam. For a moment longer Geysir dozes. Then with a roar he wakens, and with a deafening hiss, a rush and a gush, a column of steaming water is hurled two hundred feet into the air. The visitors, applauding like a crowd at a display of fireworks, let out a long "Ah . . . h . . . h!" of admiration.

Having been awakened, Geysir performs again and again for the next twenty minutes. Then with a final roar subsides, like a bored and aged lion, into sleep again, till the next week-end load of sightseers, and the next application of soap.

As well as her astounding number of volcanoes—Iceland has the greatest concentration of volcanoes in the world—she can boast of her earthquakes. Earthquakes and volcanoes belong together. Three regions of the country specialize in these earth tremblings, the most active in the southern lowlands between Reykjanes and Myrdalsjokull. Here for two days in August 1784, a quake destroyed ninety-two farm-steads and damaged half as many others. In August and September of 1896, twice as many were destroyed, a terrible loss to a country that then had a population of only eighty thousand people.

So dangerous are these earthquakes that Iceland's cities must be constructed with the tremors always in mind. In Reykjavik only reinforced concrete houses may now be raised, concrete houses deeply embedded in the earth. Stone or brick, even if easily available, which they are not, would be too dangerous.

Iceland is so rich in waterfalls and cascades that it would be im-possible to name even half of them. Three, however, are outstanding, and two of them quite easy to reach. Between Akureyri and Husavik in the far north, and easily seen from the main road, is Godafoss. Foss means falls, and this is God's Falls, so named because Thorgeir, one of the early Vikings converted to Christianity, tossed his house-hold idols into the roaring waters—perhaps to baptize them also, or to make them harmless. The falls are the more impressive because the beautifully crescent-shaped torrent rises in the grimmest desola-tion, among lava, rocks and black and gray slag heaps, with never a whisper of green in sight.

Still further north and much more difficult to reach, is Dettifoss, Tumbling Falls. Jolting, the road winds through a dreary waterless waste of lava-strewn land, birdless and plantless, where black volcanic mountains rise on every hand and the black sandy earth is alternately flat as a board, or ploughed with outpourings from some past eruption. But the Dettifoss, when you reach it, drops straight down the rugged cliffside, churning and roaring as it goes. Near Dettifoss lies the Valley of Hell, a long deep depression between the moun-tains, as bare of grass as a landing field, and strangely menacing. It has earned its sinister name because of the heavy snows that gather here in winter, making it very dangerous to travel.

More famous even than the first two is the Golden Falls, Gullfoss, about sixty-five miles northeast of Reykjavik. The waterfall is not impressive compared, for instance, with Niagara, but it is very beautiful, due to its semicircular, stair-like descent. Its crashing thunder can be heard from a long way off, and the rainbow mist that rises from it sprays out in incomparable colors on the grass of its banks. In winter daytime the shining stars above it make it even more eerily beautiful.

Many of Iceland's most spectacular falls have been harnessed for electric power, and at one time Gullfoss was so threatened. An English hydroelectric company planned to put up a plant on the site, and had made offers to purchase the property surrounding the falls to the farmer who owned it. However, the farmer's young daughter violently opposed this move. She threatened her father; if he sold to the company she would throw herself over the falls to certain death, a sacrifice far greater than that of Thorgeir who merely tossed in his household gods.

Father relented. Perhaps he knew the resolute quality of these Viking women. The falls were not sold, and the young lady, now an old lady, is alive at this writing. This is a true story, and if it had happened in earlier days it would certainly have been fashioned into a skald-song or a saga.

The central plateau of the island is mountainous, wild and barren. Where volcanic fire was once the enemy of all life, vegetable as well as animal, the other enemy, cold and ice, is now in occupation. The frigid white successor of the ancient lava floes is now in grudging slow retreat, but still occupies a tenth of the country's surface. Even in summer, pockets of snow lie beside the main bus route, and seldom is one out of sight of snowcapped hills gleaming brightly in the sunlight, their rugged slopes adorned with patches of white like strange heraldic symbols and mythical monsters. Yet in spite of the snowy appearance Icelanders sunbathe, the air is mild; the twenty-four hours of summer daylight, and almost as much direct sun, may account for this warmth. There is no night chill to temper it.

Along the coast the retreating glaciers, Nature's bulldozers, have scored the coastline to fjords and inlets that cut deep into the country, forming welcome harbors for fishermen. But the southeast coast is still claimed completely by the glaciers.

Giant crouching mountains, purple-black or copper-dark, snow stained, alive with tumbling waterfalls; such landscape has a sinister but enchanting beauty. Water, water is everywhere; streams, fosses, rivers meandering softly or rushing swiftly as the great icecap melts and pours into the sea.

Due to shallowness, or brevity, but mainly to too boisterous rapids, the rivers are not navigable, but the water is made use of in many other ways. It is reckoned that Iceland has the greatest amount of available waterpower of any country in the world. Geysers can be tapped, so can waterfalls; hot springs can be piped to heat houses and to warm greenhouses. All these modernizations are taking place in Iceland, and just as Nature is continually remaking the island's landscape, so is man refashioning it for his own use, harnessing Nature to do his work for him.

And that is fair enough. After their only war, but that one lasting a thousand years and causing heavy losses in lives and property, Icelanders believe they are victorious over their volcanic enemy. And it is the custom of victors to exact tribute, indemnity or reparations from the conquered.

It is Iceland's good luck that the Gulf Stream flows around her, washing both northern and southern coasts. It is this that makes her climate so temperate, never too hot, never too cold. Otherwise she would be as bleak, as glacier-smothered, as her neighbor and old colony, Greenland.

But it may be that this is what makes her temperamental weather. In the B.B.C. meteorological reports issued from London, the usual announcement begins, "A low pressure belt is approaching from Iceland . . ." or "high pressure" as the case may be. The Icelanders declare that such reports, hinting that all weather, and most of it bad, originates in their island, is a libel on the country. They prefer to claim that Iceland weather actually rises in the Great Lakes region, and is diverted north-eastward by the warm waters of the Gulf Stream. On the east coast of the island cold currents from the Polar Basin, encountering warmer airs from the south, create the constant fog which is characteristic of that region. Fogs along the west and south coast are rare.

Whoever is to blame for her weather Iceland does suffer from abrupt and violent changes within a few short hours, even within minutes. The forecast for the day must be the despair of the morning radio announcer. In one morning the outlook may alter completely from full sunlight to drizzling rain, from a wild wind that shatters the gardens and buffets the small trees in the park to a sudden dead calm. The mountains shine out, snow-streaked, brilliantly dark against a bright sky, then drop their veils of mist and vanish altogether. But the rains are not tropical downpours, there are seldom thunderstorms and lightning as with our own continental weather, and no hurricanes.

Lying so close to the Arctic Circle, Iceland has long dark winters when the sun rises to give only an hour or two of daylight. But she compensates for this by her delightful nightless summers, so impossible for the southerner to imagine. You may picnic, read a book, or take an excursion at midnight. For weeks on end daylight hours stretch endlessly ahead and there seems time enough for everything, whether unlimited work, unlimited leisure, or both. This odd arrangement when one day melts imperceptibly into the next and night drops no dark curtain between the acts, affects the Icelanders as it does most people, like the Finns and the Lapps, of these timeless northern lands. The islanders themselves say that they do not like to live by the clock. But who can blame them for making as much as they can out of the long summer daylight hours, to balance the dark hours of the winter months?

Iceland's mean summer temperature is 52°. This is not really cold, and the young people go hatless in pretty summer frocks and sweaters. In winter there are no great falls of snow, and there is seldom sufficient ice on the lakes to make good skating. Most of the harbors stay open all winter, the only hazard being the heavy ice floes that float down from the far north. But this is on the east coast only. With plenty of steam heat, brought from the geysers, with lots of hot water brought from the hot springs, the houses are always comfortably warm; this is true also in summer.

In fact, so generous is the supply of hot water that within sight of summer snow you may count a dozen or more flourishing kinds of tropical plants from bananas to coffee; grown under glass it is true, but warmed by Nature's own central heating.

Now that you know the facts, how would you answer your own question "How cold is Iceland?" Not as cold as New York, but not as hot as New York. In fact neither particularly hot nor cold.

No, Iceland's worst propaganda has been the icy name that those early Vikings attached to her. Such a name has been a libel on her climate down through the centuries. It's too bad she did not switch names with Greenland long ago.

2

From Piracy to Democracy

GARDAR, a Swedish Viking, is credited in the sagas with being the discoverer of Iceland. That was pretty early in Viking history, about 864, when the dragon-prowed longboats were smaller and less seaworthy than they later became. Gardar was attempting to reach the Hebrides, that lie off the west coast of Scotland, probably on a looting and burning raid, when a gale swept him off his course and he landed on the island's coast. He returned home filled with an explorer's enthusiasm for this new-found, and seemingly uninhabited land, which he named Snowland for its white-capped mountains.

With this inspiration another Viking, Floki the Raven, set out to repeat the venture. Somewhere along the course he loosed three ravens from his ship; one turned back toward Norway, one returned to the ship, but the third winged straight westward. Floki followed his name bird. This method of finding the nearest land, also used by Noah when he loosed the dove from the Ark, was a most practical one. From the deck the horizon was close, from the stumpy masthead it was still very limited; the ships were small and extremely low in the water. But a soaring bird could see much further, especially one of the great winged predatory ravens with their remarkable vision.

Floki landed on the west coast of the new-found land, the eastern coast being then as now high and rocky and filled with glaciers that poured their icy waters into the stormy seas. From a hilltop beside

18

a fjord, a long inlet from the sea, he looked down on still more ice and snow, and named the place Iceland. Unfortunately the name stuck, and has remained to malign this beautiful country for over a thousand years.

In 874 the first colonists began to arrive from Norway. Harold Fairhair had managed to unite most of Norway under a single monarch and it seemed a good chance to impose taxes on the individual chiefs. They objected, naturally; never before had anyone asked them to hand over any part of their ill-gotten gains. The Viking warriors, in rebellion against the Internal Revenue as many a disgruntled citizen has been since, with their families, their cattle and considerable wealth set off for the new world in the west in search of "freedom." They were probably the most ruthless and courageous batch of colonists the world has ever seen.

Their leader was a man named Ingolfur Arnarson who was accompanied by his foster brother, Hjorleifur Hrodmarsson. Ingolfur had been to Iceland before, and had liked the country; he had also sacrificed to the pagan gods for good luck on the voyage. Hjorleifur had made *his* preparations in a somewhat different manner; he had quarreled with and killed two sons of a neighboring Norwegian chieftain and his possessions had been confiscated in payment for the two lives. In order to equip himself for this voyage he had had to make a special trip to Ireland to loot and plunder and recoup his fallen fortunes from the gold of the monasteries. Hjorleifur was a Christian, of a rough and ready kind.

As the two approached Iceland Ingolfur hurled overboard the carved and sacred pillars of his high seat, or chief's throne, saying that he would make his home wherever the gods decreed that the pillars drift ashore. This was symbolic, the new home should be a continuation of the old. On landing the two brothers parted, and for some time continued to settle in various places, which now bear their names. Two years later Ingolfur discovered his pillars, and laid claim to a large section of land on which Reykjavik now stands. His foster brother was less lucky. In the spring he began to till land near his new house, and having no oxen, harnessed his Irish slaves to the plow. The Irishmen, who may have been of equally good blood, rebelled and slew their master. Later they were captured and slain by Ingolfur.

Colonists poured in. Each chieftain took up land for himself and ruled his own district. Such districts, called *Landnam*, landtakes, were all recorded, and their records have come down to us, so that we can tell today that about four hundred people of rank and influence (with their wives, children and thralls, who did not count) shortly settled on the land. It has been estimated that by 930 Iceland may have had a population of twenty-five thousand. Iceland, more than any other country in the world, has a full and detailed account of her beginning as a nation.

The colonists found only a few men before them. These were Irish monks who had fled from the Vikings in Ireland when their monasteries were burned and looted. They had named the island Thule. Now they fled again, to the Westman Islands, "men of the west." A few names in Iceland still testify to these earlier settlers; Papos, meaning "bishop" and the inlet of Petreksfjodur, Patrick's or Peter's fjord.

Though there is no record of them there may have been inhabitants in Iceland even before the Irish; it is improbable that the monks simply sailed out into the blue, hoping to find land somewhere at the end of the world. Ships driven off their course may have landed there and brought back news of it, and there is a story that, not long ago, two Roman coins were found on the beach. But war vessels, whether Roman or otherwise, did not carry women and families, and hence no settlements were made.

It is claimed, somewhat sentimentally, that the Norsemen left Norway in search of freedom. But the records show clearly that the only freedom the chiefs sought was to be free of greater chiefs, and that the tyranny they escaped was no greater than that which they imposed on their followers and serfs. They continued life much as they had lived it in Norway, and for a century or more still kept in close touch with the home country. It is probable that they still thought of themselves as Norwegians.

They also continued to raid. In Norwegian-built ships the Icelanders, along with their cousins the Danes and the Swedes, and of course the Norwegians, looted and plundered; West Scotland, Ireland, the Hebrides, the Faeroes, all knew their wrath and cruelty, and in the churches of Scotland there was often offered up a frantic prayer, "Lord deliver us from the fury of the Viking."

There was no lack of luxuries, and though Iceland was not so well off as Norway, she had considerable trade, in Iceland falcons, the best in the world, in polar bears, as gifts from one foreign king to another, in narwhal bone, in eider down, in blue fox furs, and in the more staple products such as fine wool and homespun, cheese and butter. Nor was there lack of manpower; slaves, called serfs or thralls, could be had for the asking, or anyway for the raiding.

These lusty warriors who had left Norway rather than submit to an overlord were unaccustomed to compromise, unaccustomed to anything save capturing by force and holding by force. Naturally they clashed. Bloodthirsty interclan warfare became the custom of the country; the sagas are full of feuds and bloodshed. Brother avenged the murder of a brother by the death of a neighboring chief or clan head; wife avenged the death of a husband, or started a healthy feud of her own, for the women were almost as bloodthirsty as the men. But a distinction must be made; the country was not in a state of anarchy. Each clan was under the rule of its leader, a leader both political and spiritual. He could arbitrate between members of the clan and, as he was usually the strongest and best fighter, he could enforce a rough and ready justice, though only within his own clan.

The difficulty grew as the population increased, and clans began to spill over from one boundry into another. Wrongs, or fancied wrongs, occurred between those on one side of the boundary and those on the other.

Slowly the clan system of government, based on the family, began to yield to a territorial system, based on where a man lived. There were more freemen; men who had broken away from serfdom were no longer slaves, and having taken up land of their own no longer gave service to a master. What was greatly needed was a series of laws and a common system of judgment for the whole of the island. Something like a federation of clans.

Many rebelled at this idea; some chiefs even packed up their chattels and crossed to bleak Greenland, for the same reason that they had originally packed up in Norway and come to Iceland. The situation on this small island was one of many independent states all refusing any form of federation or other common link.

But the link had to come. The catalyst which was to fuse the clans was the Althing. A system of *Things*, popular assemblies which somewhat tempered the rough rule of the clan chiefs, had been brought from Norway by the original colonists. Though Icelanders were not yet ready to accept, or even imagine, a chief or king over all the island, they did realize that some higher judge must be set up to pass laws, and to adjudicate between the continually quarrelsome and warring chiefs. This would be the Althing.

So in the year 927 a man named Ulfjot from a southern district was chosen to prepare a code of laws, and a plan for carrying them out. He traveled to Norway—men crossed to Norway then in the longboats as casually and comparatively as easily as nowadays we might go by plane—to seek advice. While he was away his foster brother, Grimur Geitskor, Goatbeard, was sent on a journey through the countryside to seek out a site for a general assembly. The valley of the little river of the Oxara was his choice. And none better could have been chosen.

The Althing was set up in a place called Thingvellir, Meeting Valley, about thirty-five miles north of the present city of Reykjavik.

It is a fabulous place, a fitting site for the birth of a pagan parliament. Here in some far distant past a mighty eruption had taken place, and from a neighboring chain of volcanoes the valley had become filled with a gigantic flow of molten lava. In time the surface cooled and the hot fluid beneath forced its way out of the opening where the lake now lies. A great cavern was formed. Then the roof of the cavern shrunk and during one of Iceland's many earthquakes, the entire crust collapsed, breaking away the mountain slopes on either side of the valley and forming two great parallel rifts of rock, which face each other across the wide, stream-watered plain.

In the center of the valley flows the sweet running Oxara, reflecting quietly the black mountains that encircle it; and at the head of the plain thunders a steep waterfall. The Vikings are credited with having rebuilt the rock wall here, and having led the river from the valley beyond so that their chosen place might have the water it needed. Save for a church and for a few small houses cradled in the plain, this scene has not altered for a thousand years. It is Iceland's most sacred spot, and in 1930 was made a public park.

Here, for two weeks in the summer, came chiefs from all over the island. It was the big show of the year, a County Fair, Inauguration Day, Election Day and Chautauqua all rolled into one roaring, clattering, celebrating festival. Each chief had his appointed place, a booth to which he could return year after year, where his thralls and family and freeman tenants gathered together, his skin tent was set up, his horses tethered, his meals prepared. Sheep, cattle and ponies were swapped, races were held, wrestling matches took place, feasts were given, stories and sagas sung and told.

In the early days great horse fights, a favorite sport of the Vikings, took place here. But these, by order of the Althing were finally forbidden. Not because of their cruelty, but because excitement over stallion fights so often led to human fights. There must have been plenty of athletic and martial contests, brawls over drink, and trade and women, and plain hot-blooded challenge.

There were also formal fights imposed as part of the judicial pro-
cedure. Where two parties to a dispute refused to accept the judgment of the Althing, they were often set to fight it out, standing knee
or waist deep in the running river, where they could slash and hack
right lustily till one was killed or was drowned. It must have been a
colorful, rowdy, brawling assemblage.

But the purpose of the Althing was to settle disputes, not to
stimulate them. Withdrawn a little from the hurly-burly sat what
amounted to a Supreme Court, which decided cases that did not
come wholly within the jurisdiction of any one chief. Its members,
drawn according to fixed rules from the different sections of the
island, were the only federal power uniting the whole country.

Yet more remote from the noisy crowd, like a still small voice of
justice, the law-sayer droned on. Volcanic violence, not human tools
had raised the crude dais from which man-made words sought to
wipe man-made violence from the land. The view spread out before
the law-sayer perched on his high, natural rock terrace seat must have
been an exciting sight. Immediately below him, crowded, shouting
and elbowing in the rock valley-within-a-valley jostles the select
audience of the clan chiefs, to whom he relates day after day, from his
prodigious trained memory, the accepted laws of the land.

Outstanding and impressive, these giant Viking chiefs, red-haired or
blond, heavily bearded and with long flowing locks beneath their
shining steel casques. These are the leaders of the sea wolf packs, each
man remarkable by reason of great strength or great cunning. Their
brynies, coats of linked chain mail, are especially burnished for this
occasion, and the breeze catches their long cloaks, of red and blue,
embroidered or woven in bright colors, gold collars adorn their necks,
gold bracelets circle their mighty muscled arms, loot of a hundred
great houses and monasteries. They scowl fiercely, from habit, or
mutter and growl as the law-sayer's voice rings out reciting some law
for the good of the community, but which may restrict their desire
to seize what they can, and hold what they are able.

This is the real assembly, which for safety's sake all chiefs must attend unarmed, though the common folk below could retain their swords and shields. Such a rule is a wise one, for the chiefs are a vengeful, hot-tempered breed. And if any man feels that his absence from his home, or from his small camp in the valley might invite robbery, he has a right to remain there, armed, to protect his wife and property. But in the general assembly he can carry only his knife.

By this means the people feel that they are still in control of the assembly. They retain a right called *vopnatak* "seize your weapons." If, during a judgment, a decree is passed of which the freemen do not approve they can beat loudly upon their shields with their swords, vopnatak, to remind the unarmed chiefs above that the final power remains in the hands of the people.

This is the first murmur of the common folk, the first faint far-off whisper of the future democratic vote.

Beyond the rocky cleft in the narrow valley, spreading wide across the level plain, huddle the booths and shops and stalls of the Iceland clans. Some are of rough stone and turf, some perhaps of brush, for at this date the island was not yet denuded of all her trees. Around the booths, each serving as headquarters for clan or subclan, gather the armed huscarls, freemen, bodyguard to their chosen chief. Their robes are less resplendent than their masters', but their armor and weapons are as effective. Spears, and long-handled, small-bladed battle-axes are thrust into the earth, bows and arrows hang upon them, but no huscarl would lay aside his sword.

Above the shout and the bustle rises the constant bleat of sheep brought in for slaughter, to feed this vast throng, and the rhythmic clank, clank of armorers' hammer on stone-mounted anvil.

There are women here too, matrons in their finest attire, their long plaits of pale blond hair showing their Nordic ancestry, or their blue eyes and dark tresses betraying that a thrall, captured perhaps in Ireland, was their mother or grandmother. More freely than the men they move from group to group, exchanging news with relatives from other clans from some distant fjord of the island, ordering the slaves to their tasks, and inevitably gravitating to the stalls where everything is for sale or for barter, from local foodstuff to rich loot of foreign lands as far away as distant Constantinople.

Children shriek and dodge among the throngs, shouting in their games, driving back straying goats; ponies neigh and strain at their tethers. And noisiest of all are the youths displaying their skill at wrestling, running, spear throwing, archery and in brutal combat of sword and battle-ax. Dog fights, horse fights, the shout of boys in mock battle. And from the whole gaudy bright scene rises the scent of crowded humanity, the smoke of constant cook fires, the welcome odor of roasting meat, the brawl and shift of rowdy blare and color of this great assembly in a pagan land.

From the numerous accounts of new feuds that sprang up, new murders that took place at Thingvellir, one wonders whether the assembly settled old disputes faster than new ones arose, and whether the judges ever came to the end of the docket.

This picture may act as a corrective to the impression of the Althing that is sometimes given; of a staid and ceremonious session of pompous, dignified Elders. To understand what the Althing really was, we have to keep clearly in mind that it exercised only two of the three main functions of government. The gathering of chiefs could and did make laws for the whole island; it could and did give judgment in any criminal or civil case . . . and among primitive peoples criminal and civil are the same. But the Althing had no executive functions. None whatever. It was neither soldier, police nor process-server. When it fined a man for murder it could not collect the fee. The relatives of the dead man did that—if they were powerful enough. When it sentenced someone to outlawry—a favorite form of punishment—it couldn't really throw him out of Iceland, it could only give men license to kill him if he remained. When it restored wife to husband it couldn't really force her to go back to him; though in most cases it is probable that public opinion backed up the judgment of the judges.

One favorite revenge that a chief or freeman might take on his erring neighbor was to slaughter his neighbor's slaves—thralls—serfs, whichever you chose to call them. They were mere property, even a little less valuable than the wife's weaving loom, or the farmer's favorite stallion. The freedom in search of which chiefs and warriors had come from Norway did not apply to their slaves; they were property and nothing else.

Another common method of revenge was to burn down the neighbor's house. There is a story called *The Saga of Burnt Njal* which tells us of such a happening. It was preferably done when the neighbor and all his family were cozily at home and asleep. Those turf-roofed, turf-sided houses, walled with what was almost peat, and with but a single door, were handy fire traps. For this reason the early Vikings sometimes built their houses around a spring, or water was led into the houses from a nearby source by means of a wooden pipe. Like keeping a fire extinguisher always at hand. One chief is reported to have failed to put out his fire with the contents of the huge sour milk vat, and henceforth was known as Foki Sour. After death! Of course this perilous existence hardly made for progress in trade, in farming, in other peaceful pursuits. A man doesn't get on with his work if he is always having to be wary of his neighbor, and it is a handicap if your sheep are lost because your shepherd is lying out on the moors with his throat cut, just because your neighbor thinks he has a grievance over your last horse trade.

In the year 1000 Christianity came to the island and was accepted by all. We have a vivid account of it in one of the sagas. It is told that the Christians set up their booths, and that on the following day, both sides, pagan and Christian went to the Law Rock and each side declared its former community of laws dissolved. Then there arose such a tumult on the Mount that no one could hear his neighbor. They then all left the place of assembly, and the situation seemed fraught with the greatest danger.

The Christians chose as their law speaker Hallur of Sida, but he went to Thorgeir, who was still a heathen (and was probably chosen by them precisely for that reason). He was universally known for his fairmindedness, hence his verdict would be acceptable to all. Hallur gave Thorgeir three marks of silver to proclaim what the law should be.

That entire day Thorgeir lay with a cloak over his head so that no one should speak to him. The following day, which was June twenty-fourth of the year 1000, all assembled before the Law Mount. Then Thorgeir asked to be heard, and spoke. "It seems to me that things have come to a dangerous pass if we do not all have the same law. If the laws are torn asunder, then security can no longer prevail, and we cannot afford to incur that danger. Now therefore I shall ask both heathen and Christians if they will abide by the laws which I shall proclaim."

All agreed to that.

He said that he required binding oaths by both parties that they would abide by the laws. They all agreed to that also and he took their pledged faith.

"This is the foundation of the law," he said, "that all men in this land are to be Christians and believe in one God . . . and that they are no longer to worship idols nor expose their children, nor eat horsemeat. If any man is found guilty of these practices he shall be condemned to outlawry, but if he carries them on in secret, there shall be no punishment involved." The further comment is made in the sagas that the heathen felt they had been grossly defrauded; nevertheless in a few years heathen practices died out and none practiced them.

Because the horse was sacred to Odin and its meat was eaten in sacrifice to him, the Church put its ban on horsemeat. An additional reason was of course the Old Testament ban on eating the flesh of non-cloven-hoofed beasts. Permission to eat horsemeat privately was undoubtedly intended to abate antagonism to the new law.

Many felt that Christianity was a softening religion; many opposed it for years. But slowly it took over, slaves were freed, new-born children, hitherto exposed on the mountainside if they showed signs of being crippled or half-witted, were now taken care of in the home.

There is a further story told that many of the hardy Vikings demurred at the idea of baptism. It was a cold country, baptism by immersion was the custom of the Roman Church at that date, and no husky warrior wanted to get wet all over. Then someone suggested that the rite would be just as cleansing and the vows just as binding if the baptism took place in one of the island's numerous warm springs. Whereat the resolution passed without further objection. They didn't balk at a bath of hot blood, but cold water was another thing; you had to draw the line somewhere.

Fighting, with crashing sword on clashing shield was their life, their hobby and profession. The sagas hold few love stories; almost every tale deals with fighting in some form, and Valhalla the pagan heaven was a place loud with battle, where men fought all day, cut off each other's heads, and at nightfall had their wounds healed, their heads miraculously restored, so that they might all sit down together and feast and drink all night. To resume fighting again next morning. Presumably their morning-after headaches also disappeared by magic.

The change from the religion of fighting and feasting, whose ultimate reward was more fighting and feasting, to the religion of patience, whose final reward is peace, seems almost to forecast the change in Iceland itself. From the gore and riches of piracy and unbridled civil war within, to eight hundred years of hardship and peace.

3

From Isolation to the United Nations

By 1262 the Icelanders had become weary of their incessant feuds. Also they may have begun to realize that by killing off all their best men, chiefs who should have become leaders of the people, they were weakening their own stock. They badly needed a leader, someone to act in supreme authority over the island and stop the endless quarrels. But there was too much jealousy for them to choose one from among themselves. So the people, no doubt against the wishes of many of the chiefs, sent to King Magnus in Norway, for help in their problem.

The king's treaty with Iceland was not a hard one. She should swear allegiance to Norway and in return Norway would send someone to govern her. In addition she should pay tribute in a certain amount of cloth each year. So important was this homespun wool that a length of it was considered a medium of exchange, almost a coinage, as we consider a dollar.

Thereafter life became safer. But almost immediately the Icelanders became aware that they had opened the door to the tax collector, the very cause of their original flight from Norway and Harold Fairhair. They also began to resent their loss of independence.

At this distance it is almost impossible to see the rights and wrongs of the case, as the practical gains and losses were immediately fogged by emotions both political and nationalistic. The king himself could

30

scarcely have been expected to come to Iceland and handle their problems personally. He did send his agents to sit in the Althing. Many of these agents were cordially disliked; they spoke in a strange accent, they ate different food, clothed themselves differently; no doubt they criticized the country as being backward and provincial. The Icelanders in turn must have called the Norwegians snobs, "stuck up" and "high hat." We had similar problems in America, prior to 1776.

Magnus also provided that important court cases be sent to him in Norway for trial. This also the Icelanders resented, though it is a little difficult to see how else the king could have acted, according to agreement, as judge and mediator. This too parallels exactly one of the complaints of the American colonists.

One treaty followed another; Iceland feeling that she had gained by one bargain and lost on the next one. And "bargain" seems to be what they really were, for at no time did Norway send an army to enforce its wishes, at no time did Iceland rise in revolt. But each time one side or the other failed to keep the agreement; nothing, as is the way with bargains, completely satisfied everyone on both sides, yet on the whole the history of the times shows remarkable common sense, both on the part of Iceland and on the part of Norway. These years, for Iceland, were not unprosperous.

When in 1380 both Norway and Iceland came under the rule of Denmark, Icelandic complaints began to seem more justified. The Danes at this period were not good rulers. Indeed, who were? And Iceland was not a colony, but was directly under the rule of the Danish king, a job for which he drew taxes and a personal salary from the island. The king seems to have forgotten or neglected his property for years at a time; and perhaps because the blood link between Denmark and Iceland was less direct and strong than between the Norwegians and Icelanders, the Danes thought of them more as a subject people. For centuries the Danes and the Norse had been bitter enemies.

Naturally there were all the usual complaints, of too high taxation and too slight services rendered. But here was something worse. Denmark had few resources, and could not defend her new property against the attack of other peoples . . . as Britain once defended her American colonies in the bloody French and Indian wars. So Algerian pirates descended upon Iceland and carried people off to be slaves on the Barbary coast, English freebooters ravaged the coast of Vestfjord in 1589, and in 1614 Spanish buccaneers carried away cattle and sheep.

The Icelanders were no longer Vikings, they had lost much of their old fighting spirit and anyway they had no fighting ships. Now dependent on their exports, wool and fish, they had to contend with England's wool prices, and England was much nearer to Denmark, Iceland's only market under the new rule. It was cheaper for Denmark to purchase from England than to send ships to her colony. Iceland had never been self-supporting, nor is she today.

Because the Icelanders objected to Danes in the Althing, the Althing gradually lapsed. Its powers had not, in any case, kept up with the growth of government in other countries. Local Things administered the laws locally.

It was in the seventeenth and eighteenth centuries that Iceland entered her worst period. It is a miracle that she survived so much disaster, and still retained her strong national characteristics.

Nature seemed bent on exterminating the Icelanders entirely. Volcanic eruptions followed each other with horrifying sequence. Earthquakes shook the houses into wreckage, lava wiped out whole regions of pasture land and farmland, the poison gases from the volcanoes destroying human and animal life for miles around. These eruptions not only wreaked their own local damage on the land, but affected the island's climate as well, and unusually severe winters were accompanied by ice floes and heavy snowfalls, which in turn brought floods from the glaciers in the following summers.

Three hundred years earlier, in 1402, two thirds of the population had been killed off by the Black Death, and now in the eighteenth century a third of the population was wiped out by a smallpox epidemic.

Schools and churches had been forced to close, but all through the disasters the Icelandic passion for education remained. Home teaching took over from the schools, and the Lutheran ministers refused to marry any couple who could not read or write, so that illiteracy was almost unknown. The sagas were read and reread, the poems from the *Edda* were memorized and recited on the long, dark winter nights. The love of learning was the main consolation of a people who had lost their independence to a foreign rule, and much of their means of livelihood by natural disasters.

With the sixteenth century came something that really was oppression. In addition to the taxes which had been exacted under the rule of both Norway and Denmark, taxes for which little was given in return, came a dog-in-the-manger policy of Denmark's king. If Denmark, owing to lack of shipping, and the fact that she hardly needed Iceland's fish, could not trade with her colony, then no one else should do so. The penalties for a merchant's trading with ships from any other country were extremely severe, even to loss of both hands. And for a time the mother country refused to let one district of the island trade with another. As no district was completely self-sufficient, this brought on appalling privation, as well as considerable smuggling and the horrible penalties exacted for it.

There may, of course, be another story behind this, which does not appear in Iceland's recorded history. At this time most of the northern countries were at war with each other, with short intermittent periods of uneasy peace; trading ships, as distinct from warships, were only beginning to be specialized. It's not difficult to guess that Denmark would not wish the aggressive English, or the successful Spanish, or others to establish a trading base, an area of influence and possibly even a military base, within Denmark's own colony.

There is record of considerable boot-leg trading between Scotland, her northern islands, and Iceland.

In excuse for the Danish attitude it should be remembered that the modern idea of a colony and of benevolent government was entirely unknown. Indeed that term "colony" originally meant a Roman, slave-run farm, to which only the worst slaves were committed, a sort of chain gang village, or Devil's Island. It seemed almost useless to struggle along, against such bitter hardship, famine, sickness, bad government, heavy taxes and utter destitution. Toward the end of the eighteenth century the Danish Government proposed that what remained of the population should be transported to Denmark, and settled on the Jutland moors. But nothing came of this plan.

Then in the midst of seemingly impenetrable darkness came the remarkable uplift of the Passion Hymns; their effect on the morale of the country can hardly be overestimated.

The author of the Passion Hymns was Hallgrimur Petursson. Petursson was born in 1614 and like the Christ of whom he wrote, lived in poverty and sorrow. First a blacksmith's apprentice, then a laborer, he became at last a parish pastor, and grew skilled in the use of rhyme and ryhthm by turning much of the Bible into Icelandic verse; he felt that the stories would in that way be best remembered by such people as could not afford books. Then Petursson became a leper. And began the Passion Hymns.

It is impossible in a translation to realize the beauty and the majesty of these poems in their own language, the conflict and agony of Christ from Gethsemane to Golgotha; they rank among the best religious poetry of the world. For more than three centuries these hymns were taught to the children of Iceland, and one of the hymns is usually sung at every burial. In 1914 the three hundredth anniversary of Petursson's birth was celebrated throughout the country, and the largest and finest church in Iceland now bears the name of this greatest poet of Iceland's darkest days.

There followed other great men, idealistic, wise and able, rising above the dispirited people as Iceland's snowcapped mountains tower above her plains. Among them was Eggert Olafsson, 1726 to 1768, another poet, philosopher as well as horticulturist, who stimulated the people to new hope. Also Skuli Magnusson who worked for reforms in farming, husbandry and fisheries and fought against the Danish monopoly until, in some part, this disastrous restriction was lifted. The Society for National Enlightenment was founded by Magnus Steffansson, who obtained two printing presses for the country and began to publish the first popular magazine in the Icelandic language, and many books translated from foreign tongues. All this began to prepare the country for her coming struggle for independence.

It was Jon Sigurdsson, whose statue now dominates one of Reykjavik's principal squares, who led that struggle. Born in 1811 he was a philologist, that is, a student of languages, as well as a historian, publisher and prolific writer. With great judgment as well as personal charm, wisdom and temperance, he was for many years the steadfast leader of the Icelandic people. He urged young Icelanders to acquire business training, and to interest themselves in political activities. He stood behind the co-operative movement . . . and Iceland now has one of the strongest co-op groups in the world. He also worked for law schools, for local medical schools, for agricultural training. At a time when Iceland was emerging from centuries of isolationism, and was in dire need of such a leader, they found him ready. He was progressive, constructive, and no fanatic. In this Iceland was lucky, for such a leader may, by wrongly capturing the imagination of the people, turn into a Hitler or Mussolini and the country fall into the hands of a dictatorship.

In 1874, while Sigurdsson was still alive, he had the pleasure of seeing King Christian IX of Denmark grant Iceland a Constitution which restored the Althing to its former legislative power, and gave it the control of Icelandic finances. Amendments in 1903 and 1914 also gave the country partial home rule. But she was not yet completely on her own, or completely clear of Denmark.

In December 1918, Iceland was acknowledged by the Danish Icelandic Act of Union to be a completely independent state, Denmark to be represented only by a Minister Plenipotentiary. Though King Christian X, now only a figurehead, still drew a salary from Icelandic taxes, and though he had veto power over Icelandic legislation he never exercised it. The island ran its own post office, banking and monetary systems, tariff laws, penal code and even steamship lines.

When, in 1940 Denmark was invaded by Germany the Icelanders felt that since the Danish king could no longer discharge his duties to their state, and Danish ships could no longer help police Icelandic waters, they should be completely free of Denmark. There was also the danger that if Germany won the war, they might be considered as a mere colony again and taken over by the German Government as a dependency. Cynics might say that Denmark's tragedy was Iceland's opportunity. The Althing voted to end their allegiance to Denmark, and on June 17, 1944, the birthday of Jon Sigurdsson, National Iceland Day was proclaimed, amid great rejoicing. She was completely free; her last link with Denmark was broken.

Bells on the island pealed. Parliament and some twenty thousand citizens from all over the country gathered in the open air at the ancient Thingvellir to celebrate. They voted to install Sveinn Bijornsson, of ancient Norse Icelandic lineage, to serve a one-year term as president. Thereafter they would vote for a new president every four years.

But storm clouds had gathered. Iceland was defenseless, and there was a war on.

In May, 1940, the Canadian and British troops came to Iceland. The Canadians were the first to arrive in Reykjavik, the capital. Shortly thereafter followed the British. Neither of them were received with wild enthusiasm. The Icelanders, displeased at this occupation, puzzled and sullen, lined up to watch the debarkation in stolid silence. Few of them had ever seen a soldier; in a thousand years no foreign troops had ever landed on their island. What did this mean? Had the British taken over their country? It was all too difficult to understand, so they watched and waited.

For some years Germany had been busily wooing Iceland. She fully understood the country's proud intellectual heritage; she offered the young men of Iceland scholarships in her universities, special studies in volcanic geology, entrance to ski clubs and gliding clubs. Some of the older people had been educated in German schools and spoke the language; they did not speak English.

It was therefore a little difficult for the strongly isolationist Icelander to understand why England, who over the years had sent them only a few sportsmen to fish for salmon in their waters, a few professors in English who were woefully ignorant of the old culture of the country, should suddenly seem to invade their shores.

But in every way the British troops were cordial; and correct. Guns, armored cars, entire anti-aircraft units came ashore and troops marched and heavy guns rolled through the narrow streets of Reykjavik. In a short time the small island, only two days' steaming time from the British Isles, and five from the North American mainland, was a bristling fortress, to protect from German submarines the important North Atlantic shipping lanes. With Iceland bases in the hands of the enemy, Canada's air route to her eastern seaboard would have been cut almost in two.

By early autumn the Icelandic attitude had become not only welcoming but cordial. For one thing, and long before the British troops arrived, all normal Icelandic export had ceased. There was no shipping, and her principal export, fish, could find no market outside her own shores. She was looking an economic crisis squarely in the eye.

The arrival of the troops eased this problem, the commissariats of the two armies made huge supply purchases from local sources; in addition, the soldiers going into town on leave poured British shillings and pounds, Canadian quarters and dollars, lavishly into the merchant's tills.

It was in July 1941, that the United States took over from Great Britain and at their request, the task of protecting Iceland, and our government gave the Icelandic government formal assurance that such forces "would in no wise interfere in the slightest degree with the internal and domestic affairs of the Icelandic people."

Long before the war ended there was a feeling in Congress that such overseas bases should be retained by the United States, or at least the right to use these bases, and a ninety-nine year lease on such airbases was proposed. This was as much in the interest of commercial aviation as of defense. Iceland was divided in her opinion of such a move. The strong Communistic group in the Althing propagandized for the removal of the 5,000 troops; it was significant that the huge airbase which the United States had built at Keflavik, thirty-five miles from the capital, provided the first line of defense against transpolar aerial attack on the United States from key Soviet air bases. Also, of course, on Iceland. Without access to an airbase in Iceland it would be impossible for the United States, in wartime, to ferry short range jet aircraft to Europe, and security of the North Atlantic sea routes depend largely on patrol planes based in Iceland. The small island, in Russian hands, would be a serious menace to the United States.

The older Icelanders fear that the Americans may corrupt their youth, and the purity of the old Norse language. The hour-long radio program which once a day broadcasts from the airport is said to be infecting young Icelanders with American ideas, with jazz and slang. Also nearly 2,500 Icelanders are employed at the base. The fishermen and trawlers, who in any case due to manpower shortage have to hire foreign labor, complain that the high wages paid in Keflavik by the United States government have upset their economic pattern. Though the Communists press these claims for all they are worth, they do not mention the general prosperity that the foreigners have brought to the country.

In contrast to the decline of American popularity the Russians are strengthening their position. Russia takes a large amount of Iceland's fish, and supplies the island with an increasing amount of gasoline, though at a higher price than that brought from other countries. This was the overall situation in 1954, at a time when, after Stalin's death Iceland felt that the Soviet policy toward the rest of the world might be softening.

Then came the invasion of Hungary by Soviet troops, and the use of tanks against civilians. Iceland hurriedly reversed its decision. Better relations were established between the United States troops and the Icelandic Government, work on the airbase was resumed, and a loan was negotiated to bolster the always shaky Icelandic economy.

The situation now rests on a reasonably friendly foundation. Some of the United States' officers have learned Icelandic, have married Icelandic girls, and come into Reykjavik for their days on leave or have permanent homes there. But these are only the officers on leave and in civilian dress; one never sees the American uniform in the city streets and the G.I. keeps strictly to his barren windtorn base, to his American slang, jazz, baseball and football games and imported movies. The base is a small United States town that has little or no influence on Iceland and her ancient culture. Nor has the United States purchased the land for the base; it still belongs to Iceland. Only one small portion of it was bought and paid for, that is the few square feet on which the flagpole stands. And that is the only spot of green grass in the whole of the airbase.

But the Communists in Iceland have been less successful in other directions. They could not prevent an otherwise unanimous vote in 1949 to join NATO, and Iceland has been a member of the United Nations since November 19, 1946. She also takes an active part in the Nordic Council of Scandinavian States.

After her thousand years of forced isolation, Iceland is back again in international circulation. Her new, wider horizon offers new opportunities. It also imposes new burdens and responsibilities which she shows no signs of shirking.

4

The Greenland Mystery

∞

A PAPAL MISSIVE of 1492, the year when Christopher Columbus landed in the Caribbean Islands, asserts with unimpeachable authority that "Greenland lies at the end of the world."

In the century or two just before Columbus the known world had begun to stretch out, most disconcertingly, northward and westward. And with the knowledge of Greenland the cartographers had had to extend their ideas of what the globe was like. But even then, and even to Columbus, the world was still one great land mass, the whole surrounded by an immense circle of ocean, an eternal sea. A picture not so very different, save in extent, from the old pagan Norse world in which the land mass, humped like the back of a turtle, was surrounded by a serpent holding his tail in his mouth.

Actually by 1492 Greenland's short and tragic history was ended; she had vanished into oblivion. She had been Iceland's sole colony, and for some two hundred years a most valuable colony. From that point onward her story reads like a mystery tale in which the clues are only now being uncovered, as archeologists have begun to dig in her frozen soil.

We do know who first discovered Greenland and who settled her, and when and why, for all that is laid down in the wonderful saga history of Iceland.

Eric, the hero of our tale was a red-headed boy of ten when his father, Thorvald Asvaldsson, Viking, and violent as were his Norwegian neighbors, got into trouble over a murder, and was outlawed from his farm and possessions in Norway. So Thorvald packed up his wife and his family and emigrated to Iceland. That was about the year 960, when the island had been settled for more than a hundred years. Arriving so late he found the valuable part already claimed, and took up poor land in a rocky western valley. Eric as eldest son would in due course inherit this bleak property.

As the boy Eric came of marriageable age he bettered his situation by taking a well-to-do wife, and all might have gone smoothly save for his violent temper. He was always in trouble with his none too placid neighbors, and he never took his place among the great chiefs of the island. Finally, in a quarrel more serious than the rest, he killed two sons of a nearby farmer, and the Althing decreed that he should be outlawed for three years. This was not the same as being outlawed for life, but still he had to find some place to live, Iceland was no longer his home. His friends . . . and in spite of his bad temper he seems to have kept a few . . . hid him till he could get his movable property together and escape; his plan was to go in search of an island reputed to lie to the west of Iceland.

So, in his ship, with his family, he sailed forth to that new land. Rowing along its rocky and icebound eastern coast he sought a place where he could find good pasturage and soil for farming. The eastern coast, in midsummer, would still have been enclosed by drift ice, and it must have been a most discouraging exploration. But rounding the southern tip of the island he pulled inland, deep into the fjords. This, washed by the warm Irminger current, a branch of the Gulf Stream, was warmer, greener, more hospitable. Eric deliberately named it Greenland, a good real estate agent's trick.

During his three years of exile he explored many of the other fjords. He found a bleak and rugged country, whose enormously high mountains were always snowcapped, where glaciers reigned eternally; the whole interior of the land covered by an enormous sheet of ice, burying all valleys and hills far below its surface. But along the west coast, and especially near the sea, a good supply of grass for cattle grew in the short summer, with willow scrub that would support sheep and goats. The streams and inland waters teemed with fish; seals and walrus were abundant, and the shore and water-fowl could be had for the shooting. It was not a bad country for a man who had been raised in rugged Iceland. Eric chose land and built a house, which he called Brattalid, in one of the more pleasant and fertile valleys.

At the end of his three years as an outlaw he returned to Iceland. But he was still unable to get along with his neighbors, the quarrel flared up again. And this time Eric decided that he would sail away and settle permanently in Greenland.

His sales talk was a good one, his enthusiasm for the new land was contagious; Greenland, to which he had given so enticing a name, sounded to other Icelanders a good place to go to. Early the next summer a fleet of twenty-five ships set sail for the island. The ships carried from five to seven hundred hopeful colonists with a great cargo of food, cattle, horses, sheep, tools and skin tents, a veritable Noah's Ark of humans and animals. One can easily picture the distress and discomfort, the quarrels and disagreements, the courage and endurance of such travelers in the small, man-powered open boats, as they were swept by the heavy seas between the two islands. It is no great wonder that some turned back, and that others were lost in the waves. Only fourteen of the ships reached Greenland.

The colonizers landed on the western coast, and chose places to farm.

There was among the Vikings a custom known as "passing over with fire," a pagan custom that had not died out, for Eric worshiped the old dark gods. The householder, having picked the land he wished, lighted a big fire while the sun was still in the east; a fire that must be kept burning till nightfall. Thereafter he must walk, he and his thralls, till the sun reached the west, and there light another fire. No man could claim more land than he could thus "pass over with fire."

The settlement grew. Eric became chief, which may have been his purpose all along. Colonists swarmed over from Iceland, and two groups of farms known as the East and the West Settlements sprang up swiftly. These stiff-necked Norsemen were conservative, and were never able to adapt themselves, at that time or even later, to the hunting life of the Eskimos who inhabited the land to the north of them. They fought the Eskimos, but were also intermittently friendly with them. At this period of Greenland's geological history the ice did not reach so far south as it was later to do. Hence the Eskimos kept to their northern homes, better suited to their way of life, and did not encroach on the Icelandic settlements.

Eric's farm grew large and prospered, as did those of his neighbors, some of which were able to support as many as twenty or thirty people and up to a hundred head of cattle. The cattle gave little milk per head and had to be penned during the long dark winters and fed on the hay which was hand gathered during the short months of summer. As with European cattle of this period they must always have starved during the cold months, and it is recorded that from sheer weakness they often had to be literally carried out of their stalls in the spring.

Like the Norwegians, like the Icelanders, the Greenlanders based their diet on milk and fish. Milk furnished them with cheese, and the soured milk called *skyr* which they stored in big vats. There was excellent wild fowl hunting as long as the Greenlanders had weapons; there was also caribou, walrus, and even polar bear which floated southward on the summer ice floes. Bread and porridge were for feast days, though they might have grown barley, and lyme grass made a poor kind of gruel.

The great lack was wood and metal. Ice floes brought driftwood, not enough for fuel, but often large enough for the essential door posts and bed posts. Though there may have been small copses of

willow and birch on the island when Eric found it, the unfenced cattle
would soon have cropped down all young growth, and the sheep and
goats, which roamed everywhere summer and winter, would have
finished the job. Metal had to come from Europe; though some
attempt seems to have been made to smelt bog iron, the transplanted
Vikings were not skilled smiths, and little came of it. The Greenlanders never learned from their Eskimo neighbors the use of bone,
narwhal tusks and whalebone for tools.

Unless they went on hunting expeditions further north, among
the icy fields and glaciers, the colonists would have seen little of the
Eskimos. These Skraelings, as the Vikings called them, the Skinny
Ones . . . as they named also the Indians they met in Vinland later
on, were short, squat, dark-complexioned, and physically better
adapted to this grim environment than the heavy-boned blond Norsemen. So was the Eskimo way of living, an elaborate one based on
hundreds, perhaps thousands of years of survival in the far north.
The Eskimo culture was, and is, a hunting culture. The Eskimo
lived then, and still lives, almost entirely on the country; he was in
no way dependent on metals, on grain, on wood and other materials
from the outside world.

The two dissimilar groups, Norse and Eskimo, could seldom have
understood each other, and never mingled. The Norsemen had everything to learn from his perfectly adapted neighbor on the north, but
no way of doing so. He continued gallantly, desperately at times, to
force his Scandinavian way of life upon a country too bleak to support
it. And seemed for a time to succeed.

So the Icelanders settled down and became Greenlanders. Their
houses were of stone, quite well built, with turf piled up against
the outside walls often to a thickness of nine or ten feet, to keep out
cold. The floors were of stamped earth; there was no fireplace, nor
were fireplaces known at that date among Europeans. The fire was
built haphazardly, in any place in the room that was convenient, the
smoke allowed to wander out through the turf roof as it willed. The

women worked indoors, spinning and weaving, and the long dark winters were enlivened by games of checkers, or by long recitations of the sagas. Here in the crowded common room, meals were cooked and eaten, furs or dried skins were tossed down to sleep on, and rolled up and put away in the daytime.

As in Iceland these Greenland houses often had a small stream of water brought right into the house, its course covered over by flat stones, and an outlet provided on the further side of the room.

The Vikings were a belligerent, quarrelsome race; above anything else in the world they loved fighting. And even transported to Greenland, and on a more restricted diet, the Viking breed did not immediately tame down. Raids between neighboring farms were frequent, quarrels over the ownership of cattle, of sheep, of land, even of wives, would flare up. You never knew when your neighbor might stage a raid on your homestead. And he had an unpleasant habit of setting fire to your dry turf roof and trying to roast you alive inside your own oven of a house. A stream through your living room was certainly a convenience.

Eric the Red had three sons; the eldest, Leif, was to be famous for his trip to Vinland. But before that, around the year 1000, he made a voyage to the home country, Norway. On his way he was blown off his course onto the Hebrides, where most of the people had been Christians for several generations. He became interested in the new religion, and being less stiff-necked than his famous father, he allowed himself to be baptized when he reached the court of King Olaf in Trondheim. Olaf was the greatest preacher, the most persuasive missionary of his generation, and sent bishops all over the Scandinavian world, even down into Germany, to preach the faith. If he could convert by no other means, he did so by fire or sword.

Leif then sailed for home, accompanied by a bishop, and carrying the king's command to announce the new faith. It was on this trip that he picked up a ship's crew lying helpless in a wreck. In such seafaring days it was considered extremely lucky to rescue a wrecked sailor, and thereafter Leif bore the nickname of Leif the Lucky.

But Eric, now an old man, resisted this new Christian religion with all his might, for did it not forbid fighting? And what would heaven be without its grand and glorious sword fights? Furiously Eric told his son, "The rescue of the sailors was a good thing. But this bad thing you have done cancels it out; this bad thing of bringing a Christian priest to Greenland."

Yes, that's all down in the sagas, the very words of Eric the Red, spoken to his son a thousand years ago.

Greenland was a fertile soil for Christianity, many of its colony were well educated and much traveled, and there was a lively trade at that time between the island and the Western Islands, the Faeroes, Norway, Ireland and even Denmark. The Church became thereafter the strongest bond between the colony and the courts of Europe. This was perhaps more true of the settlers around the newly erected churches, than of the farmers who lived alone, far inland. For generations the latter clung to the old dark gods, and there is a most interesting saga concerning a sorceress Thorbjorg who, clad in a garment set with glittering stones, in catskin gloves and a black hood lined with lambskin, traveled from farm to farm, much honored, and casting spells and prophecies for the still pagan Greenlanders.

But the Church grew and expanded its power and the archbishop of Greenland took on the authority of a chief of all the peoples. On the great Gardar plain a cathedral was erected and consecrated to St. Nicholas, the patron saint of seafarers. Its walls were of sandstone in mighty blocks, some of them weighing as much as five tons; its windows, framed in carved soapstone, had glass panes, a great luxury for those days. All this still lies there; the ruins were excavated in 1926.

The parish grew, both a nunnery and a monastery were established, there was training for the clerics. The bishop's house was a center for both religious and social activities; merchants were received there, news brought in by ship was spread from there. It was a busy bustling time for this island at the end of the world.

But most of the bishops seem to have missed their more comfortable home life in Norway, and to have spent much of their time away from their sees, neglecting their Greenland duties. When Bishop Alf died in 1377 no new man was appointed for twenty years. Even then, though he bore the title and drew maintenance for the position, his successor did not travel out to Greenland. In fact no bishop after this one ever again went out to the island, though right down to the Reformation there were bishops of Greenland—who lived in Norway!

There is little excuse for the absentee bishops. The years between 1100 and 1300 were prosperous ones in the colony, and there were imported luxuries, brought by a growing export trade. Walrus tusk was in great demand in Europe, in place of African ivory, which was both expensive and difficult to get. Greenland was the greatest source of walrus tusks. Scandinavian markets took it, so also did Germany, France and the British Isles. Another valuable product before the days of hemp cordage was walrus hide for rope. The hide was enormously strong, so strong that the pull of sixty men could not break it. The women spun a coarse and useful cloth from the wool of the Greenland sheep, and the wool itself was also exported. The women also made cheeses from ewe's milk. Polar bears were caught occasionally and shipped away to amuse the courts of European kings, and Greenland falcons, standing nearly three feet in height, were supreme in a day when hawking was the sport of kings. There was a plentiful, if mixed cargo to fill the small, oar-driven, single-sailed ships, which plied from Greenland.

It was in 1261 that Greenland came under the Norwegian crown, as a settlement of Iceland. A hundred and twenty-one years later the Danes took over Iceland, and with it the smaller Greenland colony. But in the meantime Norwegian sea-power and maritime trade, once the strongest in Europe, had diminished, and Greenland, which had no timber with which to build its own ships, became neglected. This seems to have occurred because, with the fading of the Viking age, came a vast change in the type of ocean craft. The Germans, through the Hanseatic League, built larger, faster sailing ships, higher in the water and requiring no rowers, so with less crew could carry a greater cargo. By the year 1300 the Scandinavian trade with her colony was almost nonexistent.

It is probable that the German ships, small as they would seem to us today, were too large for the comparatively slight trade with Greenland. So risky a voyage among the storms and ice floes was not worth the slight profit. To make things still worse for Greenland, Denmark refused to issue letters patent for ships other than Danish vessels to trade with her outer colonies.

Greenland was, however, promised two ships a year, sailing from Bergen in Norway. And for a time that promise was kept. Then the *Knarr*, known as the Greenland *Knarr*, was lost, and for years no trading ship made the long perilous voyage. Thereafter, though an occasional ship did get through or men were shipwrecked on the inhospitable eastern shores, there was almost no communication with the outside world. Greenland could purchase no wood, no iron, no cereals for bread, and produced none of them herself. Gone forever were glass church windows, and the latest fashions, fresh from the courts of Europe.

We learn what little we know about this period of the dying Greenlanders from recent excavations at Brattalid, Eric's home, and at Hvalseyfjord Church.

With the beginning of the fifteenth century the Greenlanders sink out of sight. There is no record of them whatever in the pages of history. This is a strange and unique disappearance. A whole people vanished in the chill northern mists, though their land could still be seen on a clear day by their relatives in Iceland. They might have dropped off the earth for all anyone heard about them. From time to time some Danish bishop began to plan an expedition to see how the souls of the Greenlanders were resisting heathenism; or some king, missing the taxes that he once drew from this lost colony, or wishing a new polar bear for his zoo, discussed such an enterprise. But always a political move or change of ruler blocked the effort. It seemed as though Fate herself wished to wipe out the memory of Greenland from all minds.

Greenland was well out of the path of the sailing ships of the day, but a few explorers rediscovered the island. They invariably found only Eskimos. It was in 1585 that John Davis, one of Elizabeth I's great navigators landed there. His chronicler Janes reports, "It was the most deformed, rocky and mountainous land ever we saw," and Davis himself wrote, "The lothsome view of the shore and irksome noyse of the yce was such as that he bred strange conceites among us, so that we supposed the place to be waste and voyd of any sensible and vegitable creatures. Whereupon I called the same Desolation." Later, on going further inland along the western fjords he somewhat modified this original impression. But the people he encountered were all typically Eskimo in appearance, clothing and customs; there was no trace of the vanished Norse colony, its churches, monasteries, harbors, farms or several thousand inhabitants.

Other expeditions followed. In the summer of 1607 Henry Hudson noted the eastern shore on his charts, and William Baffin, another English navigator, voyaged further north than any European explorer for the next two centuries, bestowing his name on Baffin Bay.

In 1921 Denmark sent an archeological expedition to Greenland, to try to rediscover traces of the lost colony and solve the mystery of its fate. For two centuries there had been a few Danes in Greenland but they were not settlers; they were newcomers, a sprinkling of doctors, missionaries, traders, teachers, working among the Eskimos.

These archeologists, excavating among the graves in Herjolfness, the old port of the Western Settlement, found it necessary to dig into perennial ground-ice to recover such bodies as the encroaching seas had not yet washed away. The soil had been so constantly frozen ever since burial that garments were still perfectly preserved around the bones they clothed. The few skeletons recovered were sent to Denmark for anatomical observation.

Then at long last began to emerge the answer to the mystery of the lost colony. The report on the bodies was tragic. The last of the Greenlanders were ravished by disease and want, suffering from chronic underfeeding. There had been high infant mortality, and half of these who had passed the age of eighteen had died before they were thirty. The tall, splendid Vikings had shrunk in stature, especially the women, till they were no more than four feet six inches in height, the men at the most five feet three inches. Rickets was diagnosed, and curvature of the spine, atrophy of one arm or one leg, and spinal tuberculosis. In addition the skulls displayed a very small brain capacity, though there was no trace of a mixture of Norse and Eskimo blood.

The conclusion of the archeologists was that here was a race that had been doomed to extinction, by malnutrition and too close interbreeding.

They could now begin to reconstruct the past. Various things beside the lack of shipping and of ships had contributed to the disaster, the clues could not be ignored, and they give us a picture of what really happened and how rapidly it took place.

For one thing about 1300 the climate grew colder, as climate often does change in a hundred years or so. Slowly, slowly the cold of the north crept downward; slowly, year by year, the Eskimos encroached on the shrinking farmlands. Livestock could no longer thrive in the brief bleak summers. In the long dark winters for lack of the all-important hay, cattle died in their sod and stone byres and the sheep perished outside in the snowy wastes. Except for fishing— and they no longer had imported wood with which to replace wrecked or rotted boats—Greenlanders were wholly dependent upon their cows and sheep, for they grew no crops.

Upland farms would first be abandoned, and gaunt starving men and women of middle years, who could survive better than the old and the young, must have begged the traditional Norse hospitality of kinsfolk nearer to the sea, and to hope. Yet these were in no better state. During the years survivors must have become few. Did they at last, a pitiful handful gather in the once luxurious international port of Herjolfness, with its empty homes and all but empty hopes, and gaze south and east for a ship which at last must come, must come! Or did a few Eskimos kill them as casually as one brushes off unwanted flies, these people who had failed to adapt themselves to their environment? We do not know, and we are never likely to know.

It must have been about the year 1500 when the last Greenlander died. An old Norseman, nicknamed Jon Greenlander, relates how, on one of his voyages he sailed deep up a Greenland fjord. He found houses, and on the mainland he found people dwelling. But they were all Eskimos. He landed his men on a small island among sheds and booths and stone houses for drying fish, similar to such houses in Iceland.

"There," reports Jon, "we found a dead man lying face downward on the ground. On his head was a hood, well made, and otherwise clothes both of frieze cloth and sealskin. Near him was a sheath knife, bent and much worn and eaten away; we took the knife with us as a keepsake."

It was the lack of island iron with which to construct weapons that also contributed to the disappearance of the Greenland colony. Thus passed in shrunken poverty and starvation the last of the great Norse adventurers to Greenland. It took nearly five hundred years for the news of their disappearance, and the reason for it, to reach the world.

Greenland is today reasonably prosperous and well peopled. In 1924 Norway sent over a shipload of colonists, a political move as she wished to lay claim, by right of settlement, to the northeast portion of the land. Norway placed her claim of prior discovery to settlement before the International Court at the Hague. But the claim was decided against her, the court ruling that the flag of Denmark covered the whole of the island.

Eskimo is now the universal language of Greenland, and there are no natives who can trace their ancestry back to Eric and his followers, though a few Greenlanders have a trace of modern European blood. At this time the whole of West Greenland is inhabited from Cape Farewell north to Melville Bay. The country is well administered by the Danes, churches and schools are again established, and each of the thirteen west coast districts is governed by a Danish factor; the outposts and hunting stations within each district are administered by native Greenlanders who from time to time report back to the factor. The Greenland flag is the Danish flag, with the addition of crossed harpoons.

With the occupation of Denmark by the Nazis in 1940, Greenland came under the protection of the United States, under the American-Greenland Commission with offices in New York. This now acts as a clearing house for both exports to and imports from Greenland. The United States has the right to establish air bases, military and naval facilities there. Technically Denmark has sovereignty over the area, though the United States has full jurisdiction, save that for any offense Danes and Eskimos are turned over to local authorities.

Marble is mined and exported, so also is soapstone. But the chief export is cryolite, for cryolite mines on the west coast are to date the only place in the world where this peculiar ore is found in sufficient quantity for commercial uses. The Eskimos regarded it as a special kind of ice, since it is colorless or snow-white and it melts easily in candleflame. It is a source of metallic aluminum, and is also used in the manufacture of a particularly tough glass and porcelain.

In a modern world where oil wells or strategic importance may bring wealth to a wilderness overnight, boom-towns may yet blossom on Greenlands glaciers. But it is unlikely.

Ghostly Greenland still overshadows its modern descendant. Families too tough for bloody Viking Norway settled Iceland. Those too brutal for feuding Iceland-settled Greenland. "Farming a glacier" would about sum up the impossible task they set themselves, these six foot heroes of battle with their tall blond womenfolk. They almost succeeded. They built a civilization in a chill wilderness, but failed to adapt themselves and live on the country.

The world forgot them. They died no noble death in battle, such as would carry them to the Valhalla of their ancestors. They hungered and degenerated, slowly, each year of the final centuries a painful backward step of physical misery and retreat from gallant aims. Until the last hope and the last life vanished from the ledger of history. The empty ocean lapped at their feet, and the chill mists of the north were their shroud.

5

Move Over, Mr. Columbus!

WE ARE ACCUSTOMED to thinking that Christopher Columbus was the first white man to land on American soil, and every October he is hailed as the "discoverer" of America. But the truth is that he never did find the mainland, nor did he know it was a new continent. He thought he had come around the world as far as Asia. And he was certainly not the first or even the ninety-first white man to land here. Not by some five hundred years.

Neither was that little Peregrine White we read of in school the first white child born on the continent. Nor was Virginia Dare. No, it was a boy named Snorre, and he was white, of the Viking breed. He was born here, somewhere along the eastern shore of North America, around the year 1000. In a place called Vinland. Though no one, up to now, is quite sure just where Vinland was. Except that it really existed, and was a good sound Norse settlement for several years.

It seems that a rich Norwegian trader named Thorfinn Karlsefni traveled to Greenland and stayed there for a winter with Leif Ericsson, the first explorer of America. He married Leif's brother's widow, a woman named Gudrid, and with a crew of sixty men and five women, took livestock, and attempted the first colonization of the new world. His son, born in Vinland, was Snorre.

The account of them, related in the *Heimskringla, The Lives of the Norse Kings,* is very matter-of-fact. Snorri Sturluson, who died in 1241, and who took down the old chronicles or sagas as people told them to him in his native Iceland, had no ax to grind. So far as he was concerned Christopher Columbus, the Jamestown settlement, Virginia Dare and the Pilgrim Fathers as well as other claimants for first honors in America did not exist. Nor had America any importance in his eyes.

Nor was Karlsefni the first European explorer in America, nor even its first European discoverer. The first man mentioned in the sagas is a man named Biarne, some ten years earlier. His fame came by accident. He lost his way, on the trip to Greenland.

The sagas tell how Biarne used to sail off to trade each summer, and return to Iceland to spend the long winters with his father, Herjulf. One summer he returned to find that his father had emigrated to Greenland, still further to the west, to join his friend Eric who had been the first settler there. Biarne is supposed to have warned his crew that it might be rather risky sailing to Greenland as he had never made the trip before. But his crew agreed to take the chance and they set out.

They sailed for three days, then were driven south and had fog for three days. The fog lifted and they sailed for a night and a day and saw land, well wooded, with low hills. They sailed on, keeping land to their portside; they sailed another two days and saw more flat and wooded land. Then they sailed northeast, leaving the land, for three days, and saw what they took to be an island, with big waterfalls and icebergs. In three more days of sailing to the northeast they reached Greenland, and Biarne went ashore to live with his father Herjulf. If you check by any atlas you will find that the only land southwest of Greenland is North America.

Biarne went to Norway, possibly the following summer, and told of his discovery, but was blamed for not finding out more. He returned to his father and is said to have left the sea for good. So far as he was concerned anyone could have America that wanted it.

Biarne had discovered, but it was left to Leif Ericsson to explore this new land. Leif was the eldest son of Eric, the first colonist of Greenland. Leif came over from Brattalid to talk with Biarne on his father's new farm at Herjolfness. Yes, this is all related in the records. Leif had heard of Biarne's remarkable discovery, and no doubt he wanted to go along on his next trip. But Biarne still felt the same way about America. Instead he sold Leif his ship.

Leif gathered a crew of thirty-five and asked Eric to be leader; Eric demurred. Leif argued the old man into riding down to look at the ship, but on the way his horse fell and damaged his foot. Eric took this as a warning and said, "It is not fated that I shall discover more lands than Greenland, on which we live. And we ought not to proceed all together on this voyage." So he went back to Brattalid to his other sons, Thorvald and Torstein, and his daughter Freydis.

Leif followed Biarne's course, but in reverse. He went ashore on Biarne's island "with high fells and icebergs." There was no grass; a rocky shore led inland to the snowcapped peaks. He named it Helluland, or the Land of Bare Rocks. Some think that was Labrador. It looks right, on the modern maps.

He raised anchor and sailed on, to land on a white sandy beach leading to forests, and called this Markland, or Forestland. It may have been Nova Scotia, but look at the map and make your own guess.

Again he raised anchor and pressed on further to the southwest, for two days running before a northeasterly gale, and came to a land which Biarne had not sighted. How far did Leif sail per day before this gale? We know that at this period a ship had crossed from Norway to Iceland, a distance of perhaps 800 miles, in four days. No doubt that was exceptional. Leif may have sailed four hundred miles to the southwest; or less. He landed on an island which some think may be Long Island. He towed his ship up a river into a lake and camped ashore, and there he built shacks and a "great house" in which to spend the winter.

It was a wonderful place after bleak snowy Norway, and the still more rugged Greenland. Salmon, they said, were more plentiful and larger than back home. Plenty of game, wild corn of some kind, and grapes. And above all, no frost in winter so that the grass did not wither. This, and Leif's noticing that day and night were about equally divided, have led some to believe that the place Leif called Vinland was much further south than the mouth of the Hudson. People can spend hours with dividers and protractors, and all arrive at different guesses. What we can be sure of is that Helluland, Markland and Vinland lie somewhere along the eastern shores of North America, and in that order, from north to south.

In the spring this first company of explorers returned to Greenland with a valuable cargo of lumber, much needed in that treeless land, and with grapes and vines, which they optimistically planned to plant in Greenland.

Leif's father died the next winter, so Leif inherited Brattalid and went no more a'roaming. But his brother Thorvald had caught the fever, and the next summer set out with Leif's ship and a crew of thirty. Thorvald seems to have had no difficulty in following Leif's verbal sailing directions, and landed to occupy the buildings Leif had left. He hauled up his ship, fished and wintered there.

Next spring Thorvald explored further to the south, saw no humans but discovered a store of corn left by the Indians. He returned again, and again wintered in this brother's houses, which had thus been tenanted for three out of four winters. Next spring he explored east, then north along the coast. A gale drove his ship ashore and broke her keel. He fitted a new one of American timber. They sailed east again and came to what some people identify as Mount Desert Island. There Thorvald surprised a group of Indians asleep under three up-turned canoes, and slaughtered eight of them. He was to pay for this with his life, for the one man who escaped brought back many more Indians. Thorvald retreated to his ship, but was wounded beneath the arm by an arrow, and died and was buried there. His crew made their way back to Leif's buildings and wintered there. They returned uneventfully to Greenland next spring.

It is worth noting how casually the Greenlanders had taken to commuting between Leif's home at Brattalid, and Leif's buildings in America, in what was probably an eight-oared boat with a stumpy sail which could be used only when the wind was astern. But to show that the trick was not easy, there is record of a failure.

Thorvald dead, Torstein, the remaining brother, tried his hand at exploration, and to recover Thorvald's body for more Christian burial. He took his wife, Gudrid, and twenty-five men. He spent his whole summer drifting, it was said; and returning, missed the southern point of Greenland, where his home was. He spent the winter as the enforced guest of strangers in bleak western Greenland. He died there, with many of his crew, and his host returned Gudrid to Brattalid in the spring.

Now came a bigger expedition, designed for settlement, not merely for exploration. A rich trader named Thorfinn Karlsefni came from Norway in a bigger ship, and spent that winter with Leif in Greenland. He married Gudrid, Torstein's widow, and next spring, with a crew of sixty, and five women, plus livestock—cattle, perhaps sheep —set out for Leif's buildings in Vinland. Everyone was to have "equal shares of all they won."

For a time this early colony was a success. They found a bonus of a whale that had drifted ashore and which they ate. There was no shortage of fish and game, and a bull they had brought went wild in the year-round unfenced grazing. They seem to have wintered in comfort.

The next summer, the twelfth including Biarne's first discovery of America, is noted for the appearance of native Americans. Without being asked, they brought sackfuls of fur to trade, as though having had previous experience with white men, unrecorded white men! The Indians were scared off by the bellowing of the bull, but returned later.

Very wisely Karlsefni allowed no weapons to be traded, but let the white women exchange milk and dairy products for furs. Cautiously he had a stockade built for defense.

That winter the first white child was born on American soil; Snorre, the son of Gudrid and Karlsefni. This must have been early in the winter. The Indians returned and in their eagerness to trade threw their furs over the stockade. When an Indian tried to steal a weapon a fight broke out, the Indian was killed and the others retreated.

But before the retreat, a curious incident occured. Gudrid was sitting in the doorway with her new American son in his new American cradle when a strange woman approached her. By the description she was garbed as an Indian, but had light yellow hair, a pale face, and very large blue eyes. She asked her hostess, presumably in Norse, "What is your name?" Gudrid said politely, "I am called Gudrid. What is your name?"

"I also am called Gudrid," said the yellow-haired stranger.

Her hostess shook hands with her and bade her sit down. She must have been consumed by curiosity and full of questions.

Unfortunately then came the fight outside and the stranger vanished before she could tell her story. But, taken in conjunction with the others of her tribe knowing enough of the white man's ways to bring furs, it is a fair guess that this local Gudrid was either a survivor, or a part Indian descendant of some earlier Norseman who, like Biarne, had been blown off his course. More probably a survivor, since she spoke Norse.

Possibly Karlsefni had not allowed sufficiently for the danger of hostile Indians in unknown numbers. Thorvald's encounter had been much farther north and he had brought the trouble on himself. If Karlsefni had stayed, the same fate might have fallen on his people as later overwhelmed Jamestown. But he was a rich man, and a cautious one. The next summer he cut his losses in the way of livestock, and returned with his people and a valuable cargo to Greenland. Much is known of their later life, even to where that first American boy, Snorre, is buried, in Iceland, where many of his descendants were once known by name.

But all was not yet ended for Leif's little hamlet in America. Freydis, sister to Leif and to the late Thorvald and Torstein, decided to follow her brothers' keel-ways. She is noted for having married another Thorvald, a little man, and as being a big and strong woman, "anxious for possessions and wealth." From what followed "anxious" seems gross understatement.

Her chance came when two Icelanders, Helgi and Finbogi, brought a ship from Norway and wintered in Greenland with Leif. She interested them in joining her for an expedition. She was to take thirty men, but hid five extras aboard her brother's boat; they took the exact thirty. Once again both ships hit their destination right on the nose. But immediately Freydis showed her hand, refusing to allow her fellow leaders and their men to occupy her brother's buildings. They had to build for themselves.

Her next step was worse. That winter she nagged her mild little husband into taking his men and attacking the sleeping Icelanders. She then forced him to kill all the men he had taken prisoner. With her own hands, since her men would not do it, she slaughtered the other five women with an ax.

Having thus secured all the profits of the trip she bound her party to secrecy, and returned to Greenland next summer. Her crime was discovered by her brother Leif, but went unpunished.

And now, after fifteen years of contact between Greenland and America, reported in considerable detail and with much verisimilitude, America, or Vinland, is no longer mentioned. This cannot be because Greenland was abandoned, for that did not happen for another four hundred years and in the meantime the Greenland colony was to increase to three thousand souls, with many churches, a nunnery and a bishop.

Leif, Greenland's leading citizen, inheriting from his father as first discoverer and settler, may have had something to do with this blackout. His attitude may be guessed from several things. He refused to follow up his exploration. He could not prevent others using his buildings in Vinland, but it is noted time after time that he refused to sell them. He had lost his two brothers on that unlucky coast, and his sister, unbalanced by greed, had committed murder many times over. There was something baneful about this new country which had slain four leaders, five women and thirty men, and to which no prospect of profit could persuade Karlsefni to return.

Nor, as leading man in Greenland, would Leif be anxious to lose settlers to this new country. It is likely that he set his considerable authority firmly against any further westward adventuring.

Ships and men would be lacking too. Greenland built no ships, since it had no trees for lumber and previous trips had been made in Norwegian or Icelandic vessels. Leif's own ship grew old.

It is probable that the Greenlanders often went fishing off nearby, rockbound Labrador, as Icelanders later fished off Greenland after its colonies were abandoned. But Vinland, the seductive, the treacherous, lay a long way further off. According to the recent excavations the Greenlanders didn't take long to become stunted, malformed and rickety from poor food and inbreeding; such poor stock does not furnish adventurers even had they had the ships.

There is a further link between the Norse and the coast of the New Lands. Christopher Columbus did not sight America until 1492. Yet in 1477, according to his son Fernando, he made a visit to one of the northern lands, perhaps to the Faeroes, perhaps to Iceland, and if the latter then it was the very place where the story of early discoveries still existed. Why did he go, and what did he learn?

It looks very much as though Columbus Day should be renamed Biarne Day, or Leif Ericsson Day. And that over an unknown grave in Iceland should be erected a tablet to

SNORRE, THE FIRST WHITE AMERICAN.

6

Reykjavik, Smoking Bay

REYKJAVIK combines two opposites, and seems to harmonize the two. It has somewhat the charm of a sleepy outdated old frontier town; it has the brisk determined air of a city that is going places and in a rush.

You come to Reykjavik from the Icelandic Airways airport in a few short minutes, instead of the usual long haul between airport and large city. In fact the university buildings, which the fast growing town will soon engulf if it's not careful, loom up only a long stone's throw from the takeoff of the planes, that zoom out, to all parts of the island at all hours of the long, nightless summer days.

The Reykjavik we see today is new indeed. All but the very center of the town is just emerging from raw gashed earth, concrete forms and temporary Quonset huts. But the suburbs are coming out of their splints, and the earth is swiftly healing over with bright gay gardens. It is within the lifetime of one man, and not even an old man, that Reykjavik was only a small, unimportant fishing settlement with a population of a few thousand. In the eighteenth century it counted only a hundred and seven inhabitants and up to a century ago the citizens fetched their washing and drinking water from a well in the center of the town, in buckets swinging from shoulder yokes. As late as fifty years ago its roads were mere gravel paths over which the trains of pack ponies trotted to market.

Much of the charm of those not-so-far-off days still remains. The town is quiet; no motor horns blare in the streets, no radios roar from its shop fronts, because Icelanders are courteous; no trains puff into its stations, because the island has no trains. Nor is there smoke of factories to dim the glistening windows or black the cement-fronted houses. The air is crystal clear, cool and rainwashed.

In the southwestern corner of Iceland the bay of Faxafloi faces straight west, and a ring of mountains, always snow-streaked no matter how deep the summer, protects the seaport town, which spreads itself along the fjord with a present population of sixty thousand, one third of Iceland's entire population. This is not a steep Norwegian fjord; its banks slope gently to the clear deep waters, and more small fishing villages, growing by leaps and bounds, dot its borders both north and southward. It was just by luck that Reykjavik, growing faster than its neighbors, got to be the biggest in the quickest time. Or perhaps because it had the best harbor.

Here in Reykjavik are no towering skyscrapers, nor ever will be. No great parks, just little cozy green squares, pansy-bordered, dotted about through the meandering dipping streets. All the houses have their small bright gardens, where the ten foot and fifteen foot trees among the plots of emerald grass are as cherished as the fragrant wallflowers, snapdragons and the enormous monkey-faced pansies. One expects a town without trees to be a little stark and empty but the bright waters of the long lake Tjornin, that wanders behind the principal streets, give it an air of gaiety, and a constant feeling of movement as the ducks and swans and other wildfowl go about their own particular business, right among the downtown business blocks. The ducks are much cherished and people turn out to feed them during lunch hour, and there are always a few children with bags of crumbs calling them to eat. They are of ten varieties; there is a painted board set up at the end of the lake describing them, each with his picture in both summer and winter garb. They nest contentedly and unmolested in a big patch of reeds at the west end, and

Warmed by the hot springs, all kinds of tropical plants can be raised in the greenhouses around Reykjavik.

Akureyri, chief town of northern Iceland is famous for its modern cathedral which towers over the harbor.

The Lutheran Cathedral. Oldest church in Reykjavik.

Land without trees, but lots of sheep.

Each farm child has his own sheep to raise.

Hekla exploded violently in 1947.

The great falls of Gullfoss (Golden Falls) is spectacularly beautiful.

In great modern drying sheds, fish is prepared for the markets of the world.

Iceland's own fishing fleet in the harbor of Reykjavik.

The Westman Islands make a picturesque harbor on the south coast.

The volcanic rocks of Lake Myvatn are like crouching
monsters. In their shadow shelters a host of wild water-fowl.

Glaciers and rough seas make the east coast inaccessible to ships.

Glaciers cover one eighth of Iceland's surface.

The eider duck, half tame and guarded by a scarecrow, sits on her down-lined nest.

Children, like so many eider ducks, sport and learn to swim in Iceland's many warm swimming pools.

Akranes, one of the modern fishing villages outside Reykjavik.

Thingvellir, the valley of the Thing, where Iceland's parliament was born.

quack and dive and paddle as gaily as though in their wild state. This is Iceland's only zoo, and it couldn't be fairer to the creatures in it. Any duck can upwing and fly away at any moment he wishes to. Few of them seem to.

It is in one of these numerous little green parks that the great Christmas tree is erected each winter, perhaps the only full size, even giant size tree that young Icelanders ever see. This is an annual gift from the city of Oslo in Norway to the city of Reykjavik, and is received with honor each year by the mayor himself. It blazes with decorations and electric lights throughout the grim winter season. That is one advantage to be obtained from midnight darkness at Christmas noon; you have an excuse to light your Christmas tree all day as well as all night, and against the Northern Lights it is a glorious sight indeed.

As usual in Scandinavian cities there is an abundance of statues, favorite sons in gray iron Prince Alberts each proffering to the public a rolled iron bundle of some forgotten law or bygone benefit bestowed, or with hand held high to greet the hurrying citizens, or just standing about, being statuesque and impressive and a little pompous. But to offset these somewhat dull gentlemen there is the heroic statue of Ingolfur dominating the town from one of the heights overlooking the harbor. He is truly magnificent as he leans on the gigantic prow of ship, his great sword which he probably called Brain-splitter or Leg-biter or some other charming Viking pet name, swinging at his side. He wears, beside his chain mail brynie and steel helmet, an expression of stern concentration on the task in hand—which was the colonization of Iceland.

If you wander down the hill, or up again along the narrow principal street . . . far too narrow now for modern traffic . . . you'll find most of the shops still old-fashioned and small, but there are big plate glass windowed emporiums sandwiched in between, and a dairy or a bookstore in almost every block. The city has over forty bookstores. Month by month, almost week by week, Reykjavik is hauling herself up to be one of the world's notable cities. Make no mistake about that.

All the newer buildings are of concrete, this is decreed by law since 1915, and is due to Iceland's predilection for earthquakes. The buildings are light gray, whitish, or almost black, and might be monotonous but for the variety of their architecture and the charm of their roofs, which make a pattern from almost any elevation. The roofs give the color to the town, red tile, tin painted green, copper, slate or wood-shingled, even a few shed roofs still retaining their grassy turf. And always the parks and the mountains and the water everywhere, lending beauty and variety to the scene.

Another such park is faced by the country's largest hotel, the Borg. This is slightly Victorian and stuffy, but comfortable enough. Across the corner from the Borg stands the Parliament House, where the Althing meets, a dignified building in Danish baroque. The beautifully proportioned interior houses the offices of the fifty-two members of the two chambers of Parliament. Further up the hill stands the national library and the fine new building of the National Theatre, which was started in 1928. Its backstage arrangement and greenroom, its modern revolving stage are as up to date as anything in New York. The theatre seats seven hundred, and has been host to traveling companies from all over the world, even a group of dancers from China, opera from Germany and Norway, visiting companies from the United States and from Russia. An opening night at the National Theatre is as gay and as diamond-bedecked as opening night at the Met.

Reykjavik has no railroads, but it has plenty of taxis, good ones too . . . and you do not tip the taxi driver. It has big new busses also, of which it is very proud, and the automobiles are everywhere, and of a bewildering international variety. Parked alongside each other, all in a row one may check them off. Cheek by jowl, their glass windows gleaming in the sunlight sits a German Opel, beside a three- or four-year-old American Ford; a Buick, a little large and self-conscious next to a square cut Swedish car; two scooters, and an English MG; then an Italian bubble car; a stern uncompromising Russian Yak, and an English Landrover . . . to name just a few. And here, as everywhere in Iceland one sees incredible quantities of jeeps, American jeeps leftover from the American military camp. On the narrow and rough country roads these sturdy little cars may bounce and jolt their passengers almost out of their eyeteeth, but they do manage to make the journey as no other car can do.

In all there are over eighty varieties of cars in town, which must be a headache for the repairman.

Except for the exported fish which is often shipped directly from the harbor of its origin, Reykjavik handles most of the island's exports and imports. It does it with little ostentation. The harbor is full of ships, mostly Icelandic, and named after the country's principal great waterfalls. The docks are as clean and as conscientiously tidy as the city streets.

The houses along the roads leading out of town, the blocks of concrete flats and apartments are as modern as in any Midwestern city; they are convenient and bright, but not picturesgue. To discover the unusual you must roam the narrow old streets that radiate out from the docks and harbor. Here you will find the little two-and three-story corrugated iron houses, characteristic and unexpectedly charming. Yes, corrugated sheet iron, that flaunting abomination! But not in the Icelanders' hands. Necessity has forced them to adopt it, but they have adapted it, made it their own. No rusty patches show through the Dutchneat paint, no two houses are alike. In their hands it is as tractable as thatch or shingles, brick or masonry. Corrugated iron facing was the nineteenth century's answer to earthquakes in a country where wood for building was unobtainable; it was cheaper than imported lumber, which of course had to be used for doorsills and doors, windows and such. Curiously enough wood never seems to rot in Iceland, perhaps because there are so few gnawing insects, or because the temperature remains so moderate, never very hot, never very cold.

But to make up for the effects of the warm branch of the Gulf Stream and the harbors which never freeze, Reykjavik suffers from some of the most eccentric and temperamental weather in the world, and heavy rains, high winds and devastating gales. The winter blasts are boisterous, often they are bitter cruel blizzards. Even in summer these gales may suddenly swoop down on the town, beating flat the gardens, whipping the small trees in frenzied punishment. Then too, there is the long winter darkness, when the only sun, if it shines at all, is between half past ten in the morning and half past two. But from late May till early August there is no real darkness, you can read if you wish all night long without turning on the electric light. The tenor of life is slowed, there is plenty of time to play, to stay up till three A.M., to picnic at midnight, or to work in the garden as long as you wish.

The autumn and spring produce wonderful sunsets, and in the winter the Northern Lights flashing across the heavens are a nightly and wondrous spectacle.

To balance this odd rearrangement of time, modern Reykjavik is blessed with enormous quantities of almost free heat and free electricity. Outside the town swift Iceland rivers, rushing to the sea, have been harnessed to furnish the power for all this lighting . . . and how much it is needed, how well it is appreciated by a people who can still easily recall the days of little brass whale oil lamps and horse tallow candles! The central heating too goes on all summer long.

It is hot water, piped from thermal springs, which since 1933 have been purchased by the city. Schools, public buildings, apartment houses, office buildings, two-thirds of the city is heated by this inexhaustible hot water. This ample supply of hot water is ably made use of in the town swimming pools. Very pretty they are too; simple, unpretentious, open to the sky, and in constant use during all the summer months. One half the pool is allotted to the younger children, for lessons and practice. For in the Icelandic school curriculum swimming takes an important place, and no child of eight or nine is allowed to advance into a higher class unless he can swim, or has an excuse from his physician. Incidently the Vikings, being a race of sea warriors, were proud of their ability to swim, even in their chain mail brynies, so the Icelander has made no great break with tradition. Though the modern child is not required to paddle in full chain armor.

It was the women of Iceland who first discovered a use for this bounty of nature, unique to Iceland in all the world. Throughout all southern and western Iceland these hot springs bubble and gush and steam . . . Reykja means smoke, and Reykjavik is the bay of smoke, or smoking bay. Escaping steam must have led the early settlers to discover the blessing of this constant flow of hot water, and even in Viking days women began to carry their washing to the edge of some stream where the heated spring furnished a perpetual supply of free hot water.

And so it continued for a thousand years. Till in 1930 the men, not the women, decided that this blessing was too good to go to waste. Water was brought in with originality and engineering skill to heat a swimming pool, which is still in use, to heat a public school and a few private houses. Then in 1943 a huge plant, still in use, was started to heat some eighty-five per cent of the city. Now, as Reykjavik is increasing so rapidly, another even larger plant is in process of construction.

And Reykjavik is still growing, stretching out like many another metropolis to gobble up its neighboring suburbs, and even outlying villages. For instance it is only a short distance to Hafnarfjordur, the old harbor and fishing village. But already houses seem to line both sides of the road, which is marked with yellow-painted stones to act as guide when the land is snow covered. These houses are all built by the owners themselves, and hence bear the charm of Icelandic individuality, a personality that development-houses, all rubber stamped from the architect's office, cannot possess. One has an outside stairway, another has three gables, another owner-builder has added an upstairs porch and has painted his roof yellow because his neighbor's roof is green or red tiles, or even slate, and has started his garden with tiny conifers instead of flowers. Almost all gardens are filled, in July, with towering lupines and low pansies and even a few roses, which are brought indoors for the winter.

Allotment gardens too are everywhere. For each school child is required, during the holidays, to cherish a vegetable garden of his own. This is excellent training, and helps supply vegetables for the home table. Somehow a few flowers sneak their way in among the sturdy potatoes and rhubarb, and like the house gardens, these mundane garden patches are often ablaze with bright poppies, roses and snapdragons, all abloom at once.

The fishing village of Hafnarfjordur lies plumb in the center of great radiating spokes of drying racks. Here hangs in the sunlight the fish which form a large per cent of Iceland's produce and export; her gold mines. Two or three times they are hung out doors. Then back they go into the drying barns where they are as neatly stacked as cordwood, pale as ivory, almost odorless, scrupulously clean; cod, herring, stockfish. All being prepared for export to various corners of the globe, each lot cured to fit its own special market. Those going to Jamaica are twice dried, fish for Italy three times; fish for Portugal markets is prepared a little differently from that for the markets in Spain. Now the salt for curing them comes chiefly from Majorca, but Iceland has found that her own sea salt will do the trick, and has begun to establish home salt ponds, as a new industry.

Do not look for picturesque little "fishing villages" in Iceland. Save for the great drying racks that fan out from the towns along the coast, and the huge airy sheds in which the dried fish is stored, there is little difference between an Icelandic fishing village and one inhabited by farmers only, except of course for the smell. The small sod and stone house near Reykjavik now used for a museum, though historically a fisherman's home, had a garden, pens for sheep and a stall for a cow or two, very much like a farmer's home.

It is probable that from the earliest days fishing and herding were so often done by the same person, fisherman keeping sheep, or having their wives do so. Farmers along the coasts and inlets undoubtedly went out to fish to augment their meager diet. So no distinctly separate pattern of housing and living developed for these two crafts. And nowadays the fisherman's houses in the suburbs of the city might belong to any prosperous farmer, small-holder or tradesman.

Icelandic fishing waters are the richest in the world. This is due partly to the two currents, one warm and one cold, that flow into her piscine pastures. The Irminger current, a branch of the Gulf Stream, nearly surrounds her, while an Arctic current flows down from the north to strike her eastern and northern coasts.

The national income is so dependent upon fishing, and the fleet fishing and even the fish-runs, upon Iceland's capricious weather, that meteorologists are at work day and night, recording, predicting, and issuing radio bulletins. Land-based planes scout far to seawards, and ships use sonar and ship-to-shore telephone to detect and announce herring runs. Ships in harbor are at constant alert, and fish-curing hands leave bed, table, dance or movie the instant news of a catch is telephoned to shore. Everything possible is done to increase efficiency and to leave little to chance. But fishing must still remain a gamble of ships, lives, and time against a finny fortune hidden in the sea, which may be here today and gone tomorrow.

The fish come to spawn in February to May in the warm waters off the south and southwest coast, and as the eggs hatch they drift with the warm stream northward to the cooler waters, where the young can find more fattening food. Maturing, they again come south to warmer water to spawn again. The flow of the currents and the quantity of plankton in the waters is watched carefully by the fishing industry. As a result Iceland's fishing catch per capita is among the highest in the world, forty times that of the European take.

Cod is the most reliable of all the fish, the standby of the industry. With whitefish, haddock, halibut and others, the catch amounts to over four hundred thousand tons a year. It is the herring, the island's second most important catch, that is temperamental. One season the herring catch may be from two to three thousand tons, more than twice that of Alaska and the United States combined, the next year it may drop to less than that number of barrels.

Icelandic herring is the finest, the fattest in the world, and contains more calories than any other known food. Its oil is used in soap making, in medicine, in margarine, its waste serves as fertilizer and is used for cattle feed. And everyone eats it, whether salted, smoked, spiced, pickled or otherwise prettied up for the market.

One of the fishing industry's main problems is manpower. In the long days of the summer vacations boys pour out from the university to work on the boats, hundreds and hundreds of them. The fishing fleet also makes do with much imported labor, from the Scottish Isles, from Ireland, from Germany and Norway. Iceland is underpopulated, and even for the farms has to bring in manpower from outside.

This, though a handicap to the country, is one of her chief charms to the visitor; that nothing is crowded, or hurried, or overdone. But it is a delicate balance for a country to maintain, that hairline between a population sufficiently strong to keep it prosperous, and an over-population without sufficient jobs to keep most of the people occupied most of the time.

She is branching out industrially to many fresh fields. Reykjavik has a new factory for concrete and an unique type of house insulation based on volcanic dust. This is light in weight, comes in big gray blocks, and is mixed with the concrete before it is poured. Iceland is already beginning to export this useful product. The material for her own cement is now dredged up from deep in the ocean off Faxa Bay, and the chalk-like material that makes the insulation comes from the whaling fjord of Hjalfjordur.

Another industry, now well beyond the experimental stage, is that of the State owned and privately owned greenhouses. One of the greatest of these is at Hveragerdi, which the American soldiers disrespectfully called "Hurdy Gurdy." Here, heated by the natural steam which is furnished by acres of geysers, acres of greenhouses glint in the sunlight, and here is raised much of the vegetables on which Reykjavik feeds. Parsley and lettuce, of course, and tomatoes and cucumbers, but in addition experiments are being tried with coffee, with melons and bananas and pineapple, and even with such extremely tropical fruits as grenadilla, grapefruit, lemons and rose cavendish.

Reykjavik is a city of hills, and each hill seems to display its own particular jewel of architecture. One of the proudest is the new home for aged seamen, which overlooks the harbor in three directions. It is as up-to-date as any resort hotel, and any hotel would be proud to claim its gleaming steel kitchens, where great stews and roasts and huge bakings are produced every day; its bright sunny game rooms where the old men can gather for chess and checkers, and whatever card games are the Icelandic equivalent of canasta and bridge. It has a fine library, and a beautiful bedroom for each old captain to sleep in, not too far from the sound of the sea; it has motion pictures, radio, and lest the retired seaman may feel homesick for his home on the bounding deep, the floors and walls are decorated with motifs of fish, seals, walrus and other nostalgic reminders. The gardens outside bloom with enormous pansies and wallflowers. The whole place breathes beauty and contentment, and is Iceland's tribute to those sea captains who, throughout her history, have kept her island trade alive. This building, like the three modern university buildings, was financed by State lotteries.

On still another hill, close by the university, stands the museum. Here everything is beautifully arranged, and for a country without great wealth, that could not afford to preserve its antiquities but had to use and wear them out, there is a remarkably fine collection of old Iceland craftsmanship. Here you will see the charming little wooden food bowls, many of them with the initials of the owner, and delightful treasure boxes, gift from some swain to his beloved, in which she could store her small jewels and ornaments. There is also a fine display of old costumes of the country, though there should be more of these.

As a reminder of the Viking sea-wolves from whom the peaceful modern Icelander is descended, there are rusty shreds of chain mail, which once glittered imposingly upon heroic chests, single and double-handed swords, daggers and battle-axes, not all innocent of blood in the tribal and family feuds so vividly described in the sagas.

On the top floor is a gallery of good local paintings and of the very modern sculpture which seems to appeal to the Icelander (Jonsson's work is in a separate museum). But the most interesting collection is in the basement, examples of the early craftsmanship of the islanders. Here are three charming pony saddles for women; the Iceland women did not ride astride, not even sidesaddle. No, they sat the sedate little horses sideways as though at home in their own rocking chair, their trim little feet in those sealskin slippers demurely planted on a small board that depended from the saddle. Behind the rider's back rose a firm support of heavy wood and leather like the back of a chair, in many cases beautifully decorated with hammered brass in a design of birds and flowers, and the letters of initials of the loved one. For it is obvious that these saddles are the affectionate work of some ardent swain. The rider traveled sideways to the road, not facing it. The whips also are handmade and homemade, and as individual as the saddles.

There's an interesting display of blacksmith's tools too, and a particularly fine show of small boats, and early craft of several kinds, as one would expect in the museum of a seafaring folk.

Iceland should begin to collect more of her old-time tools and examples of her early crafts. Little now remains of the Viking era. But it is not too early for her to start collections for her future museums; what was grandma's trash and banished to the attic or dust heap becomes granddaughter's treasure, and deserves a place on the museum shelf.

It is a pity too that none of the museum displays are labeled in English, French, Spanish or German. Nor does a pocket Icelandic dictionary prove of any value when it comes to translating descriptions, since the operative word is likely to be obsolete, and so omitted, just as "frow," "strickle," "snaphaunce," "gorget" and "niddy-noddy" would be missing in a popular American dictionary. Another drawback is the very short hours during which the museum is open, only two or three afternoons a week. From the tourist's point of view it is difficult to fit these hours into a tight schedule of sightseeing. Perhaps —and it is more than a perhaps—Iceland isn't very keen on tourists.

Reykjavik is proud of her artists. Nor do they have to die in order to be respected and recognized. On another of the city's high hills stands the beautiful home and gallery of the sculptor Einars Jonsson, a gift of Iceland to her most honored artist. He was born in 1874 in the bleak land near Hekla, and even as a boy his talent was appreciated. He studied in Denmark for many years and evolved his own style of work, strongly mystical and religious in character. In 1917 he came to the United States where he had been commissioned to execute the statue of Leif Ericsson, which now stands in Philadelphia's Fairmount Park. Another copy of it, outside the Reykjavik gallery gazes off across the bay, westward toward Greenland and Vinland that he tried to colonize.

The charm of Reykjavik is cumulative, it grows on one. Its gardens filled with bright flowers and cherished lawns, its blooming rowan trees sweet as heliotrope, its efficient and friendly bookshops, its steep little streets and amusing little coffee shops, the pond where the lively wriggle-tailed ducks dive and chatter and gobble the crumbs you throw them, the delicious ice cream in the neat little dairies, the bustling little taxis, the stern iron statues and green green parks, the clean blue skies and the kindly courtesy of everyone. All these will remain in your heart long after the plane has carried you home again. It is a city with a flavor all its own, and you come away hoping that it will continue to prosper, yet never never lose the delightful character that makes Reykjavik like no other city in the world.

7

Bleak North Country

But Reykjavik is not Iceland, the Icelanders will tell you. No more than New York or Chicago or San Francisco is the United States. You must travel north if you wish to see the country and learn about the people.

There are no railroads, no stations with which to punctuate your journey. The only way is to go by bus, and break your trip with a stop-off of a day or so at various spots along the route. These are the ones that the people themselves use, and like the buses, they are comfortable and convenient, though they are planned for the Icelanders' own travel, not for tourists. You'll go as the people go, eat the food they are accustomed to eating, sleep in the same kind of beds, though you may not, if you travel in summer, wish to stay up all night as the Icelander does. You won't have that long dark winter in which to catch up on your sleep.

The first stop-off will be Bifrost, a few hours' trip north along the lovely coast road. It is a treeless country, the grass as green as that of the Emerald Isle. The road skirts the shore, with low green hills sloping down to the deeply incut fjords. This is the most fertile corner of the island, protected by the mountains to the east and washed by the water of the Gulf Stream to the west. But do not expect to see a patchwork of ploughed fields, of rye and grain and oats and corn neatly separated by tidy fences. This is grazing, almost pastoral, country, and the basic crop is grass, to be processed into wool, mutton, horsemeat and dairy-products by sheep, ponies and cattle.

And all around rise the mountains, black, copper-toned, snow-streaked always. In the glow of late evening, the pale greenish-yellow moss that clothes the rocks gives back a golden light, and rivers dart and meander and gush and roar throughout the land, so that the road is always crossing small bridges, or skirting a stream, and the bus travelers exclaim and point out to each other a waterfall, which is sure to be noted for its height, its volume, its beauty or its historic association, above the numerous other falls. At least each region has its own famous waterfall, and what seems to be a waterfall fan club is obviously right here on the bus. These narrow west coast fjords received no sun during the four months of winter, though since the Gulf Stream flows north of them, they do not freeze. When, in early spring, the sun first touches the tips of the encircling snow-capped mountains there is great rejoicing, almost a feeling of personal triumph and release. And when the sun finally reaches long fingers down to touch the house roofs there is a holiday, with cakes and feasting, neighbors called in and a special ritual pancake is served, stuffed full of cream.

At Bifrost is a small modern hotel, built by one of the co-operatives which make up such a large percentage of Icelandic organizations. It is one of several designed primarily for Icelanders on holiday . . . and how the young people do flock to them! In the summer months Bifrost is jam packed with busfuls of girls in pony tails and bright sweaters and duffle coats, hatless in the sunny air and running two by two over the short crisp green turf. Groups of young men roar up on motor scooters or motor bikes, hatless also, with crew cuts and Norwegian sweaters. Every week-end of holiday time there is a dance, and the vacationing young Icelanders, working during these months on the nearby farms or on fishing fleets along the coast,

troop in for a gay time. They are a fine healthy lot, the girls tall
and with splendid figures, the boys oddly Irish in their appearance.

Bifrost is not planned for tourists, not for foreign tourists anyway,
but as in all the other small inns and farm hotels around the island
you are welcomed cordially, and in the English language. But you
must be willing to accept conditions as you find them, and as the
Icelander himself prefers them. The beds are narrow, hard—usually
a small mattress over bare boards, and the short quilt, the plump
eider-down comforter stuffed into a giant pillowcase, which is used
instead of a top sheet, takes a bit of practice to subdue. You turn
over in the night and the thing is on the floor; you clutch for it,
keeping your eyes tight shut against the brightness of the summer
midnight, and it eludes you, you fumble for it on the floor—then
tuck it tightly around you, and in an hour it's off again, with a
fiendish life of its own. You end up under a covering of your own
coats and sweaters, which are less agile and slippery. But the trick
can in time be mastered, you can even get to like it!

The food at Bifrost is excellent and perhaps less typically Icelandic
than further along the tour. What do Icelanders eat? It is outside of
the city and its hotels, that one first begins to get true Icelandic food.
Though even in Reykjavik little attempt is made to pander to the
taste buds of the tourist.

First there is always coffee, hot, strong, fresh brewed and excellent.
A true native will consume up to forty cups a day. Coffee is drunk
all round the clock, before breakfast, at the meal, midmorning, at
lunch, instead of tea at teatime, for dinner, and at odd times in
between. You can take it with milk or without, with sugar or without,
and it is quite correct to hold the sugar lump in your teeth and suck
the coffee through it. Breakfast, besides coffee, gives you bread,
cheese and porridge. In the country places it is usually black bread.
Not many Icelanders eat eggs, and bacon is almost unknown. Lunch
and dinner vary little from each other; fish, which is excellent, as
it would be, of course, is usually fried or boiled, the rhubarb soup

is characteristic and very good. The meat is boiled mutton, lamb or beef, but is not served in any cut that you will recognize. Mostly it is boiled and in chunks and, of course, there are boiled potatoes. Often potatoes both boiled and fried. There are no green vegetables, and what is called a salad is usually a limp lettuce leaf reposing on the hot meat. As all lettuce is greenhouse raised, it is a real luxury. So too is the parsley used as a garnish.

The thing that would be most noted by the American traveler is lack of salads and of any green vegetable. Potatoes take their place. One would think that turnip tops, or the humble dandelions which grow in such glorious profusion along every roadside, would be utilized. It is said that the ancient Vikings ate dandelion greens, but somewhere along the centuries this habit was dropped and the Icelander is not experimental. Nor has he learned the use of the mushrooms which grow profusely in some sections of the country. What grandfather didn't do isn't done today either.

No spices are used, and little seasoning of even salt and pepper. Perhaps the Icelander's palate is so unspoiled and his appetite so good that he does not need these added flavorings. Most universal of all characteristic Iceland dishes is skyr. This really is delicious. It is a soured milk with a lemony flavor all its own. The true islander eats it for any meal, with or before his breakfast porridge, with water or milk and sugar, and for a dessert after lunch or dinner, with cream and sugar. It is also very good with berries, or with peaches or other canned fruit.

Everyone drinks milk, and the ice cream sold in Reykjavik can compare with the best. No fruit is raised on the island, rhubarb takes its place, rhubarb boiled up with figs, imported; with apples, imported; with canned peaches, imported. Bread is served only at breakfast, and with the soup at lunch and dinner; when the soup plates are removed the bread is snatched from the table.

Icelanders have never had a large variety of meat, and fresh meat before refrigeration, or in the farm country was rare. The killing was done in the autumn, because hay was scarce, and once the surplus livestock was eaten there was little more meat until the next seasonal slaughtering. For this reason as well as for its great plenty, fish is preferred, and many odd kinds of sea-life were eaten in the old days; whale meat, walrus meat, seal meat, or seal flippers which were pickled in a sourish jellied loaf; and fish, dried very hard, torn off in harsh narrow slivers and spread with butter to be chewed fine. In starvation years Iceland moss and lyme grass were used in place of barley porridge. Nowadays the government is experimenting with grains that will mature quickly, in the short summer season.

The farms are widely scattered. This is because so much of the land is waste, uninhabitable, or not fit for cultivation, or will not even grow grass. On the twelve hour bus trip north up the more fertile west coast between Reykjavik and Akureyri, Iceland's second town, there are less than a hundred farmhouses to be seen from the road, and on those wide flat treeless plains one can see for many miles. The average modern farm consists of a two story dwelling house of concrete, painted cream, a few scrub rowan trees, and a little fenced plot for a small garden of rhubarb, potatoes and cabbages. The big concrete barn may hold as many as twenty cattle, and there is often a silo. Grass is used for silage here. There are a few stone sheep pens and a small shelter for the farmer's mechanical equipment.

Then the road goes on and on. Grass, more grass blowing in the wind, hosts of buttercups and dandelions and the little white headed cotton grass, with flowering wild thyme and occasional heather in the stonier bits. There is no church, no school, no other house in sight for many miles, no humans, no young people. Only the ponies, their long tails and manes tossed by the wind, only the sheep skittering away as the bus whirls past, and the snow-streaked mountains over-topping the green plain.

The young people are flocking to the towns. This is understandable, such desertion of the farms is occurring all over the world; it is a universal problem. But the young people of Iceland, who may go to

Reykjavik to study in the winter, do return to the farms in the summer. It is part of their State-sponsored education that they either do farm work in the summer months or work with the fishing fleet.

One of Iceland's loveliest spots is Lake Myvatn in the north, where, oddly enough, there is warmer and more settled weather than in the southwest city of Reykjavik. Here the usual starkness of the treeless landscape is broken by low willow scrub, and the smooth clear water of the small lake is dotted with volcanic islands, each a cone that blew its top in the general local upheaval of some four hundred years ago, when the lake was created. Many of the islands have already formed soil and are beginning to green over with grass and moss, but the black, topless cones against the bright sky of midsummer are fantastically beautiful.

The lake is haunted by thousands of birds; the most exciting are the flocks of wild white whooper swans that cluster like foam on the black volcanic sandy beach of the western shore. In midsummer hundreds of mother ducks, trailing their plump duckling babies in their wake, dive and fish throughout the long bright Arctic night.

You can take a boat, and passing through the clouds of gnats that rise literally like a mist from the shore waters, row out to one corner of the lake. Here gigantic shaggy rocks, torn and twisted by the upheaval of the explosion so short a time ago, rise from the still waters, or crouch low in it like Scandinavian trolls that the old gods have magicked into immobility. And from every shore rises the fog of midges. They do not bite, but they are annoying to the visitor who has unwarily arrived without an insect repellent.

Eastward from Lake Myvatn for some sixty miles the road runs through a veritable country of the moon. Bleak, desolate, without a blade of grass, volcanic, black and sterile, or copper-colored, or even purple, till one's eyes long again for green and growth. Great hills arise on either side, the road winds and winds; here are the marks on the ground where an airplane has landed, the grassless earth flat as any landing field need be; or there, from vents that pierce the hot ground, jets of steam arise, as though a company of underground factories were hard at work.

When again green begins slowly to appear along the roadside the eye rejoices. It is amazing how a couple hours' passage through dead land has made you long again for fertile pastures, even though they are utterly treeless, even though they are without houses, and are peopled only by the usual scattered flocks of grazing sheep. In the old days, before bus travel and good roads, a pony track passed through this grim and desolate country, and even today it is still used in winter by a few intrepid Iceland farmers who need to cross the high plateau. There are six-foot-high cairns of piled stones on either side of the road to mark the trail, a trail that would be obliterated in bad weather by blown snow. This marks as a rule the triple ruts of a pony track, made by farmers riding horseback with two pack ponies. As far back as early Viking days the farmers would have traveled in much the same manner. In spite of being so far north, Iceland fortunately has no very deep snows or sub-zero cold.

It's a long run from Bifrost to Akureyri, Iceland's second largest town and again a seaport. This is the center of the island's manufacturing, her dairies, her co-op textile mills, soap and dentifrice factories, coffee roasting and quick-freezing plants. All these are co-operatively owned; so too is Akureyri's hotel KEA, owned and run, as is Bifrost, by the Iceland SIS.

For Iceland, like her Scandinavian sisters, is strongly co-operative. Through the co-ops she purchases in the foreign markets; through the co-ops she collects and sells her milk and dairy products both locally and abroad, as well as her fish and meat and their side products. There are also co-op building societies. Anyone can join such a group, which is in no way controlled by political affiliations, religious views, or union membership; anyone can resign at any time, and anyone, whether a member or not, can trade at the co-operative stores. But only the members reap the benefit of the profits, which are shared among them.

Akureyri does not look like an industrial town. Its power is all electric from the harnessing of the many surrounding waterfalls, though it has no hot springs like the South. Like Reykjavik it is without smoke or noise, it has pleasant little parks, and even a group of trees that it proudly proclaims a "forest," as well as a pond where swans and ducks bob and dive and sail serenely. But the first thing you'll see, overtopping the town, and the last thing you turn to gaze at as you leave for the eastern shore is the church, which dominates both land and seascape. It is not large, but it is so high above the roofs of the town, its two slender airy spires pointing like fingers to the sky, that nowhere are you unaware of it. It is, of course, Lutheran, and an excellent example of modern Icelandic architecture.

This is a favorite place for the citizens of Reykjavik to go to for a short trip and rest. They say that when it rains in Reykjavik it is sunny here. And perhaps vice versa.

Travel eastward takes you now into wooded country, and for the first time you begin to appreciate how your eye has become accustomed to the starkness and austerity of an almost treeless landscape. To be sure this is not real forest that covers the mountains, but dwarf birch and willow are a pleasant change. And at Hallormsstadur is one of the four government forestry stations. You'll read more about that in the chapter on trees.

Close to Hallormsstadur is a school for girls, a pretty white building with the characteristic three-gabled architecture. Here some forty girls study, during a two-year period, concentrating on domestic science, embroidery, and especially weaving.

The only accommodation for travelers is at Egilisstadir a "farm hotel," a farmhouse that has been extended to accommodate some twenty visitors. The rooms are small, clean and comfortable, the meals are as Icelandic as you wish, English is spoken, and there is a real flavor of the country about this place. The large, by Icelandic standards, and prosperous farm on its rich bottom land beside the fjord, is comforting to the eyes after the marginal hill farms and bleak grazing lands further to the west.

There are three ways to get back again to Reykjavik. You can hire pack ponies, camp for night after night beside or on top of a frozen glacier that is perched precariously atop a volcano, and so travel for two weeks through a treeless grassless country, bleak with black lava and blue ice. Or you can take the bus. This is a two-day trip and is almost as uncomfortable as the pack trip. The final choice is the plane, which leaves the airport daily and almost immediately after its arrival. At any time during the summer it is sure to be daylight, so far north is this, and the height of the flight gives one added hours of sun.

It is an experience both beautiful and exciting to wait in the pale light of predawn, which is actually midnight, listening for the far-off hum of the engine. It taxis in, you climb aboard with no more ceremony than boarding a bus. And almost instantly you are off again, rising nine thousand feet above this barren rocky inland country. The pink of sunrise softly brushes the highest of the snow-streaked peaks. Then the first outline of the glaciers appear; there are four large ones on this route, and they can be viewed from both sides of the small plane.

From such an altitude the outline of a glacier appears no more formidable than the first icy crystals forming on a pond in an autumn freeze-up, until you realize that that spot is a volcanic cone, four or five thousand feet high. More volcanic cones appear, hollows in hills which exploded four thousand years ago—give or take a thousand or so—and having blown their tops are filled ignominiously with a few handfuls of snow. Long shadows cast by the slowly rising sun emphasize these circular sunken valleys, some of them miles in width; mountains of the moon in their grim barrenness and sterility.

Then the glaciers themselves spread out to left and right, their blue ice glittering coldly as they empty with the June warmth into tiny streams that wriggle and twist and foam, as though in desperate haste to escape to a more placid fjord and the warmer sea.

More than anything else this trip southwest across the length and breadth of the island emphasizes how large a proportion of the land can never be farmed. Not, at least, for hundreds, and perhaps thousands of years. Whether ores of value to the country, or oil, or some other source of mineral wealth as yet unsuspected will be found here as in our own Alaska, no one can predict.

The purchase of Alaska was once derided as "Seward's folly." There was some talk of Congress buying Iceland from Denmark, as Alaska was bought from Russia. But don't mention this to Icelanders. They believe that they have a hidden wealth greater than uranium, gold, or oil. Something that no money can buy, since to them it is priceless.

It permeates the whole island from the violent volcanoes to the grave deliberations of the Althing.

It is commonly called Independence.

8

Land Without Trees

In Iceland the need for more wood, for forests of any kind, is as acute as the need for water in the Sahara Desert. When the Vikings reported back to Norway on their first return trip they said that the new-found land was "forested" right down to the shoreline. Though there may have been trees of a sort, "wooded" would have been a better description. Since the retreat of the last Ice Age and the great glaciers, no conifers have grown on the island, though wood embedded deep in the rock proves that in earlier days the land was covered with such trees. But that, of course, was long before the Vikings and their optimistic reports on the real estate.

The Norsemen, accustomed in their day to a land of almost limitless big trees, accustomed to building only in timber—even their churches were of timber—accustomed to big open fires in their smoky houses, were extravagantly wasteful of their natural resources. Also they brought in flocks of sheep which increased yearly; goats as well, and cattle and horses. Sheep are notoriously detrimental to forest land, they browse down the small seedlings, so that no natural reforestation can take place; goats are even more destructive. And over a period of time all wood was used up. Houses had to be made of turf, there was no timber for ships so that no ships for trading could be built in Iceland. Wood for fuel was very scarce, and the Icelanders began to use peat, as is done today in Ireland.

Worse even than the hardship due to lack of wood was the result on the life of the people themselves. Think about it for a moment; what is the effect on a country and its inhabitants, particularly on the men, if for nearly a thousand years they have no raw materials with which to make things? The Vikings found no ores to smelt; they were not in any case particularly good with metals, though later the Scandinavians, finding excellent iron, became extremely proficient with it. They had never worked with stone in Norway. Wood was their main resource, for everything from shelter to household utensils.

All over the world a boy begins his training as an artist or as a craftsman by whittling a piece of wood into a shape that amuses him, a bit he has picked up on his path, or found beside him as he sits and watches the flocks. He may fashion a small musical instrument, or a crooked staff to hold back his sheep, or a club, or a toy sword or hobby-horse or other playthings. And, as he grows into manhood, all over the world, his start in engineering is in building, usually with that easily worked and easily available wood. He selects it, cuts it, joins it, carves it into beauty; he develops a feeling for stresses and strength through his use of it. His start in mechanics is also made through wood. With posts as levers, with wooden rollers which, through the centuries evolved into wheels, with wooden gearing to harness water power for watermills, he progresses step by step, from sled to cart, from spindle-whorl to spinning wheel. Stonework almost always follows work with wood, it does not come before it. And even work with stone needs some wood for beams, for rollers on which to shift great rocks, for inside panelling to keep out cold, for doors, shutters, window frames and such.

Lacking wood as a raw material there is no substitute, for the child who wishes to experiment, for the man who wishes to invent. Rock, grass, water, mud, the only resources of Iceland, are limited toys for the child; and for the grown man who wishes to educate himself they are even more limited. He cannot, with grass or mud, adapt old forms to new purposes, or produce outright fresh inventions.

Since for lack of ships the original settlers had to abandon piracy, Iceland's main products have been fish, sheep, cattle, and some valuable export in eider down, and a small low-priced trade in skins and furs. None of these requires very elaborate processing or the invention of labor saving shortcuts; their preparation for market has altered little in eight hundred years. The women's jobs, such as spinning and weaving were, for a time, almost the only crafts that produced anything to export, and these were carried on, from grandmother to grandchild, in almost the same way. As the centuries advanced such homespun and home weaving could not compete with low-priced machine-made cloth from other countries. Flax, which the early settlers raised here, died out; cotton never grew. And the island produced few dyes other than those pretty, but somewhat somber shades, that came from seaweed, lichen and low growing plants. Iceland in modern times never seems to have developed cottage industries, such as Harris tweeds, Scottish and Irish woolen and linen cloth. And this too may be due to lack of inventiveness. Wood for looms must have been hard to find as the old ones wore out; even the early ones wove only narrow cloth.

It is possible that the island needed more of a trade outlet to stimulate such products. The cottage industries, fine homespuns, laces and linen goods of the Scottish Islands found a sale in England, and still do, long after machine goods flooded the market. Iceland, isolated by her lack of ships and by the Danish rule, had no such easily available market.

But it was wood that was most lacking. With wood the peasant carves and whittles his household utensils, spoons, bowls, chairs, clocks and cradles. He ornaments as he carves, he works out new designs for a lighter, stronger table, for more convenient chairs, sets rockers under a cradle, and, since what soothes baby soothes grandma, sets rockers under a chair as well. The elaborate Swiss clock with its wooden cogs grew out of this household tinkering, and with such experimentations the Swiss people today are the world's best makers of fine instruments and watches.

Toys for children evolve from wood. And what the man doesn't think to fashion with his pen knife, the woman will think of for him. A better comb with which to card wool, a slight improvement for her loom and her wool wheels. The Yankees were a race of carvers, and hence the "inventive" Yankee; it was wood whittlers who finally evolved the prairie schooner, and settled the West; who built the clipper ship and sailed round the Horn. And remember the ingenious New Englander and the thousands on thousands of wooden models of inventions that he has poured into the United States Patent office in Washington. Whatever would *he* have done without wood?

Among the original Viking settlers, craftsmanship had been developed in Norway to an unrivaled extent in the construction of the tough, delicate Viking longboats. This ranks among the world's finest shipbuilding; not even today could their overall skill be challenged at this type of work. But Norway, where such ships evolved, was a heavily wooded country, so closely forested that the giant trees restricted farmland, and the young men took to the seas to plunder because their own small fields could not support them. Many a Viking warrior must have used the knife that he carried always at his belt to whittle and carve, during the long wearisome voyages, the beautiful intricate designs that wreathed his furniture, writhed along his doorposts, his bedposts, decorated the bowls he ate from, in fact almost everything that he used that was made of wood. The original Norwegian Viking was as much a "whittlin' fool" as any whaleboat sailor out of Nantucket or New Bedford, and for the same reason, lots of time on his hands, a knife in his fingers, and a plentiful supply of wood to play with.

But once in Iceland all this craft work was discouraged by lack of raw material. Apart from limiting the development of art and mechanics, the shortage of wood soon became apparent in the still more important housebuilding and farming. Without good roofing beams, roofs must shrink in size, from the great banqueting halls of the days of the sea warriors to the width of the small turf farm roofs, which is that allowed by small sticks. Even the size of drift wood recovered from the beach was limited to what could be carried inland on pony back. Sod roofs do not support themselves; they need timbers to hold up the turf.

In the summer, life could be lived outdoors, but in the long dark winters the congestion in these tiny houses was inevitably a limitation on all but the most necessary activities inside the home.

How remarkably this lack of wood has influenced the daily life of the Icelanders would be difficult to overestimate. Take sports. There are beautiful examples of ancient skis in the museums, yet for centuries skiing almost died out. For lack of wood? Quite probably. As a sport, skiing and modern skis have had to be reintroduced from abroad. Swimming was an art in which the Vikings excelled, even when weighed down with chain armor. Yet the art died out in Iceland, where the water is no colder than in Norway. For lack of rowboats and rafts on lakes and fjords? Today as we have seen, swimming has been reintroduced as a sport, and all children are now being taught in the schools.

Pleasure boating with oars, sails or outboard engines, so extremely popular in Finland and even Norway, with its dangerous coastline, is almost unknown in Iceland. Lack of wood makes it necessary to import boats ready-made, and such things are costly. Boats must be used for strictly productive work; for fishing, not pleasure.

It is when we come to farming that we realize the all but impossible conditions imposed by this lack of wood. Not only for barns, which needed extensive roofs to house the cattle, but for carts, for ox yokes, for implements of all kinds. And above all—and even today, for fencing.

In Scotland and many other places where hedging and wood fencing is impossible, stone fences have taken their place. In much of Iceland the stone seems to be unsuitable for such building. Whatever the reason, there are, save for a few localities in the north, no long dry-stone walls winding out over the moors. There are only small enclosures next to the cow byres. Without fences, sheep have had to range in common and every autumn there must be long, time-wasting round-ups. What is worse, everyman's land is no man's land. There is little incentive to hold back erosion, which is going on at a rapid pace, by planting trees, if your neighbor's sheep are going to nibble the new planted saplings. And without fencing, pasture-management, that is avoiding undergrazing or overgrazing, is impossible. Though that at the moment is not an Icelandic problem. But without fencing to keep sheep separate, nobody is going to bother to improve his stock by the practice of selective breeding.

Things are changing now. As in the American West, the barbed wire has come to stay; it allows more land to be marked off, and protected for gardening and haying, it allows the owner to keep his sheep to himself, encourages him to drain bogs, and perhaps, even more important, to raise more of the precious vegetables, which the Icelandic diet needs so badly. But fences need wooden posts, since iron and reinforced concrete, both imported, are too expensive for general use. And again we come back to that forest problem.

What is the Government doing about reforestation? It is going to be a long, slow process, due partly to the Icelander's conservatism, and partly to the climate. In Hallormsstadur in the province of Skogarvellir in the extreme northeast, is the largest national forest in Iceland. But it is small, covering only some five or six acres. Here the baby seedlings are started, and from this experimental station each year some two to three thousand seedling trees are distributed to farmers about the country. The experiments are interesting and extremely intelligent. Various trees might be coaxed to grow in Iceland; but such trees as the scrub willow, the rowan and the birch are natural to the soil and the terrain, so that the first planting is almost always of these. Using these as native foster-mothers, as windbreaks and protection, the delicate young seedlings of foreign trees are planted out. The Colorado blue spruce, brought here from heights of nine thousand feet or over; the Siberian larch, which does fairly well inland, but is not so healthy near the sea; the Danish and Kamchatka willow, and again from Colorado some fine examples of the bristle-cone pine, said to be the oldest known tree extant, specimens of which were growing in Colorado four thousand years ago. It is very slow growing. They have brought from Sitka Alaska a northern cottonwood which is quick to reach maturity.

The whole acreage is as international as any in the world; in fact since 1903, when the nursery was started, almost every kind of tree that might be likely to grow on the island has been experimented with, and from lands as varied as far-off Siberia and nearby Norway.

Unfortunately all these trees grow here much more slowly than in their native soil. The largest tree on the grounds, about fifty years old, is only thirty-five feet in height. It may be the long, dark winter that stunts them, it may be that tree culture is against Nature here. But it will be a long time before Iceland can afford real lumbering, or use her trees for any other purpose than to halt erosion, and to spread more seedlings through the countryside.

The work in the nursery is largely done by girls in their vacation time. Throughout the summer they plant the tiny seeds in the great flats, transplant the seedlings, tirelessly weed them and set them out between the protective birch and willow. Some twenty girls are thus employed, and the nursery finds no difficulty in getting helpers, there are always more volunteers than there is room for. It is all excellent training, better preparation probably than would be an equal number of hours spent in learning hand weaving, since once acquired, the love of trees and of growing things never quite vanishes. And a knowledge of reforestation and of the urgent need for it in the denuded Iceland is one of the most precious things the girls can take home with them.

Yet the great enemy of the trees in Iceland remains the sheep, the sheep which are her second largest crop, next to fish. Without the sheep she could scarcely continue to exist; but without restoring her eroding mountainsides she cannot continue to raise sheep forever. To the trained forester sheep are more dangerous than wild animals, they crop down every small precious seedling, especially the fast growing larch. If the farmer wishes to raise trees there is no alternative, he must fence out the sheep.

And to fence out the sheep from his trees he must raise trees for fence posts!

One amusing solution has been suggested. That is the Forest Dog. There is no more intelligent dog in the world, no dog more easily trained than the Iceland dog. In the old days he was taught to guard the hayfields and keep the sheep from entering. It would be quite as easy to train him nowadays to guard a plantation of seedling trees. Perhaps some day some farmer will try it.

All this lack of wood and the wherewithal for invention and experiment, combined with the extreme stress laid on literacy and books by the heritage of the sagas, has had an interesting effect on the character of the Icelandic people. There is no illiteracy in the islands, there has been little for a very long time. Probably less than in any European country. But there has been far less craftsmanship, weaving, carving, building, inventions and improvements, all of which lack grows out of the scarcity of wood over the long centuries when the island was marooned for lack also of ships.

Icelanders are rushing to make up for this. They have not, in the past hundred years, been an untraveled people; nowadays some seventeen thousand, a vast proportion of her small population, go abroad every year, to travel, not to settle down. They see what other countries are accomplishing, appraise their ultimate goals, and bring home ideas to use on their restricted island.

But the country is still very conservative, her history has made her so. Her people, though descended from the doughty Vikings, are now somewhat unadventurous, and her long inward search for culture and the liberal arts has led to a reverence for genealogy and the past, rather than for crafts, manufacture and competition in trade. Yet now she sees the need for change, and change in a hurry, to catch up with the fast changing world. Perhaps World War II and the flood of young English and American soldiers helped bring this to her attention; perhaps the danger to her independence, first from Nazi Germany, now from Russia; perhaps the need to industrialize and produce exports, to balance her economy.

Yet she does not like the change. She has not, like some countries, insisted on turning back the clock, and having all her children taught a dying language, and *only* in that language. But as far as the language is concerned she would prefer to have the clock stop where it is, or even where it was at the beginning of the mechanical age. She refuses to admit to her vocabulary modern words such as bicycle, radiator, telegram, telephone, and many others if she can concoct Icelandic equivalents based on thousand-year-old Norse. Only reluctantly does she admit technical and scientific terms of medicine, engineering and electronics. She will not even accept the Danishized terms, which often stem from the Anglo-Saxon, for it is in England and America that the greatest amount of such experimentation and research goes on. All scientific journals elsewhere carry much the same international vocabulary; Iceland refuses to.

On the other side of the coin; perhaps nowhere else in the world will the traveler meet a more likable and agreeable people. The Icelander is, to his cost, not aggressive; he has too much dignity, too many mental resources to feel that your new-fangled notions are necessary to him, or to feel that he must convert you to *his* beliefs. He has an enormous stoic patience, bred on an island which has suffered great hunger, devastating volcanic eruptions and hardships of every kind, so that he can bear with such small irritations as you may cause him. He has the three basic traits of a gentleman, courage, courtesy, truthfulness. Such qualities grow rare. Iceland is a treasure house of them.

9

More Early Settlers

THEY came by sea, they came by air. But the sea voyages must have been on ice floes, and the air transport must have been privately owned and feathered.

We mean the birds and beasts that now inhabit Iceland. For unlike the large continents, Australia, the Americas, Africa and Europe, Iceland has no signs of prehistoric animals, nor of man himself. No human or animal bones, no petrified footprints, no arrowhead or remains of kitchen midden or shards of broken pottery have ever been turned up by the farmer's careless plough. And when the Vikings arrived—and the earlier Irish gave the same report—they found only one kind of mammal on the island. That was a small fox, its fur variously dark gray or black, or red, or bluish.

How such creatures ever reached Iceland is a mystery, unsolvable as are so many Iceland mysteries. Perhaps they did come on a floating iceberg; the land was too newly emerged from sea and glacier for it to have developed life forms distinctly its own, as Australia has done. The foxes must have lived on birds and the abundant birds' eggs, and even on fish.

Early colonists from Norway brought over pigs, which have never done well; pigs don't like cold weather. They also brought sheep, cattle and goats. And, of course, horses. It is the ponies and the sheep who have taken over Iceland; it belongs to them, they are even more at home there than the Icelander himself.

The ponies are so called by the tourists; they are known at home as Iceland horses. They were brought from Norway as much for food supply as for transportation purposes. For the early Vikings ate horse-flesh—it was one of the customs they were pledged to relinquish when they became Christians—and horses, being sacred, were sacrificed to Odin. Before battle, before the launching of a ship, a horse was killed and some part of it burnt for the gods. The rest made a fine feast for the Vikings themselves. Then for centuries no horsemeat was eaten, that is openly, though it is probable that the farmer in his years of bitter poverty did not reject a meal of this abundant supply so near at home. Nowadays horsemeat is again eaten in Iceland, as is it in France and other European countries. It is also shipped abroad to be canned for dog food. Larger than the Shetland pony, the Iceland horses have altered little since the early days. Sturdy, round buttocked, they come in all colors, from black, roan, tan, cream, down to pure white, and spotted circus fashion. With their long handsome tails streaming out in the wind and wind-rumpled manes they are enchanting as they gallop wildly over the wide green moors, or frisk playfully beside the road. And like the dogs and cats and even the pretty girls they all have remarkably thick hair.

The farmer, even on the modern mechanized farm still could hardly get along without his horses. When the roads are closed to his auto, or hidden beneath drifts of snow, his small pack train can get through. The excellent modern roads often follow the old pack trails and as you whisk past in your car you can see, graved centuries-deep in the grass verge, a three or four way track. These are the ruts worn deep by hundreds of years of hardy Icelandic travel; a farmer on horseback, followed a little to the right by his relief pony and from three to twenty pack animals. Even across the sixty miles of bleak black plateau country in the north these trails can be traced; even across the glaciers that cover the northeast, the trail leads southwest

to the harbor and the city, a two weeks trek on pony back with never
a farmhouse or shelter to break the vast birdless silence. These ruts
proclaim the fortitude of the Iceland pony, and of the Icelander
himself.

Still more than the ponies the sheep have taken over Iceland as
their own. You see them everywhere, on the plains, ranging up the
high bleak mountains almost to the snows. They too are vari-colored,
from black through rusty brown to cream and white, and their fleece
is so long it hangs down in flounces and seems to follow them behind
like a woman's billowing long skirts, as they race away from the road
and the passing traffic. Junior, scuttling behind Mother, is almost
as furry, and the pale cream ones in their fuzzy coats comically resemble new hatched baby chicks.

Iceland wool is famous for its long staple and high quality. In old
Icelandic weaving the pattern was made by using the natural browns,
cream and blacks of the wool itself, not by dyeing. In the early days
the sheep were not sheared, the wool was pulled off, and to some
extent this custom is still followed, though the government urges
modern shearing.

That about covers the farm animals, save for cattle and chickens.
The cattle are of fair size and many colors, and must have been here
since the colonist days, since the sagas so often mention them, and
much of the staple Viking diet consisted of cheese and soured milk.
Their horns were used for common drinking cups, and later for pow-
der horns. There is at present no very distinct Icelandic breed of cattle, some are black and white like Holsteins, and some brown and
white and very like Guernseys. Attempts to improve the stock by imported bulls have been disastrous, as a disease to which the home
breed had no resistance carried off many herds. Now such organized
improvement is done by breeding within the herds themselves since it
has been found that the home cattle are better adapted to the country
than any other.

One sees few hens, perhaps because the winters are too dark and cold to make poultry raising a paying proposition, and chicken does not enter into the modern Icelandic diet to any extent. The farmer prefers wild fowl eggs, gathering them from the nests, then boiling them for fourteen seconds, which seals out the air and preserves them for future use.

The Icelandic blue fox may be a menace to the farmer's chickens or young lambs; still more to his eider ducks and their eggs. But the foxes are not plentiful enough to do much harm as they have always been hunted, either with bows and arrow or with knife, because of their beautiful and valuable fur. Now the farmer-hunter tries to capture the young and bring them up at home, later selling their skins for a good price.

Next in importance to the farmer, after his sheep and his horses, is his dog. It is unlikely that he could farm without this most useful animal. He is of a breed peculiar to the island, as individual as the other creatures of this strange northern land. Brought from Norway as far back as the ninth century he looks halfway between a spitz and a sheepdog, with pricked ears, a rather short snout and a tail that curls up over his back.

He is no mere hanger-on and household pet. For centuries he has guarded the lambs from foxes, herded the sheep, protected the hay-fields from the sheep themselves, guided the pack ponies along the deep rutted trails, protected the house. He is an honored member of the family, and knows it. But there was one time in the history of the country when dogs had increased at such a rate that they outnumbered the humans, and either ate food necessary to their masters, or most miserably starved to death. They also carried a terrible disease from the sheep to humans. Then many were slaughtered, and a small tax was put on all dogs. Nowadays dogs are not allowed in Reykjavik, which is probably happier for the dogs, since for animals so suited to their job and environment city life would be a most unsatisfactory existence.

The singular pureness of the Icelandic breed is due to several things.

From the earliest days no dogs have been imported into Iceland, either legally or illegally, save a few pets in the south and southeast. The farm valleys are very isolated from each other, and the dogs were trained sheep dogs, and as a rule stayed pretty much on their job on the home farm. If they traveled at all, it was only with the pack trains, where again they had a job to do.

Of recent years the Icelandic dog has been recognized by the English Kennel Club, is sometimes shown in dog shows, and an Englishman now living in California has made many trips to the island to seek out pure types of the breed, and, taking them home to his own kennels, is trying to restore the strain. Let us hope he is successful. It would be a pity if this handsome, well-mannered and remarkably intelligent breed were to die out or become mongrelized.

Just as Iceland is famous for her plague of gnats and mosquitoes, she is famous for her bird-life. One follows the other. The birds find more food than they can devour, some living on insects, and some on fish which live on insects and some, like the falcons, on the birds which live on insects or fish. As they are protected by law they migrate here to breed, summer after summer. The island's most famous bird is her falcon, which in the Middle Ages was an important export. It is a truly noble bird standing three feet high and un-disputed master of the air. At the time when falconry was a sport of kings, the king of Denmark issued orders that only he should own these gerfalcons, and used to send a special ship to bring them to Denmark, and presented them as gifts to other kings. The birds are caught young, in their nests, and so trained that they will come at a call to the gloved hand of the falconer.

In the middle ages falconry was so popular a sport that the higher clergy had a special dispensation to wear their hunting garb beneath their robes during the celebration of Mass. They were even permitted to bring the hawk to church, where it perched on the lectern.

The early Icelandic flag carried a white falcon on a light blue field; one may still see it on occasion. Then the king of Denmark decreed that the flag must be a variation of the Danish flag, which it is today. The royal bird is now used on the stars, crosses and ribbons of the Order of the Icelandic Falcon, the only official decoration in Iceland, the insignia being of Iceland blue, bearing a silver falcon. It is conferred as a great honor, upon outstanding men and women, and consists of four classes; the Grand Cross, Grand Knight of the Star, Grand Knight, and Knight, a magnificently beautiful decoration, and worthy of the master of the Iceland sky.

Along the coasts of inland lakes, you may be puzzled by the strange rafts of piled twigs and water plants. These are the nesting places of the Whooper Swan, and they congregate in hordes along the shoreline, so that from a distance they resemble a shifting border of white foam. They are heavy, awkward and slow fliers, rising to follow their leader in a wedge-shaped flock, and trumpeting to each other in deep bass notes. This may be the origin of the swan song legend. A formation flight of such impressive birds, once held royal in England, is an exciting sight, with a fairy tale quality of its own.

The rollcall of water birds is indeed a long one; mallard, pintail, teal, Barrows golden eye. The guillemots and nurres choose a shallow ledge on a high sheer sea cliff to lay their eggs and on the lower grassy slopes the puffin digs a long burrow with his orange bill. And then there is—or rather was—the Great Auk. It is rumored that he stood "as high as a man," and that he was a large edition of the penguin. This is not true. In the first place he wasn't so big, and in the second place he wasn't a penguin. He has vanished from the earth and only a few mounted specimens and his eggs remain, in museums. He seems to have been Nature's attempt to fashion a sort of Arctic penguin out of a puffin, the real penguins living in the Antarctic. Anyway he was alive and flourishing right up to the early nineteenth century, a wingless bird that did at least resemble the penguin in that it walked upright. But as to its size, it was only about thirty inches tall, not so large as the famous Iceland falcon.

The origin of the Great Auks is another Iceland mystery. In their final stage they couldn't have evolved here; there wasn't time for that, since the last great glacier covered the island. And they couldn't have flown here, since they had no effective wings. How then did they get to Iceland? And why did they ever lose their wings?

Once in Iceland, they had an unhappy time of it. They nested in rocks and crevices, and not being able to fly were an easy prey for foxes, boat crews and such vandals; then, too much hunted, they finally existed only on one of the remote Westman Islands, and about the time that Iceland passed a law to protect The Great Auk Nature took a hand, and the island blew up in a volcanic explosion, taking all but a few puffins with it. The last specimen was shot by a hunter who said he thought it was a witch.

Most valuable of all the birds is the eider duck, which plays a large part in the country's economy. This duck is almost tame, and many farmers keep a flock of them, for their soft down alone. The mother duck, to line her nest, plucks the soft down from her breast. Once the pretty olive eggs are laid, the farmer collects the down, moving among the nests without disturbing the birds; the mothers are too busy at this time to notice the hunters. Usually she re-lines her nest and the second crop is gathered by the farmer after the young have flown.

The drake, a gorgeous creature, is most devoted while his mate lays the eggs; he stands beside the nest conversing or making soft, consoling quacks. But once the hatching period is over he feels his duty is done, and makes for the nearest eider duck club, among his fellow drakes on the rocking waves well out at sea. During the later summer season the drakes moult so heavily they cannot fly, and the young mothers, tending their young, become a mere shadow of their former selves. But once the young are grown and able to fend for themselves, the duck and drake are reunited in wedded bliss.

Iceland's most historic bird is, without doubt, the raven. The sagas are full of him. When Odin was alive, a conquering chieftain at the mouth of the Danube, he was said to have owned two ravens who served him as scouts, and would return to perch on his shoulders to whisper to him the latest reports on the enemy. When Odin came north to Sweden, and was deified, his ravens also became sacred, and were known as the symbols of battle and death, as omens of victory or defeat. When the first settlers brought Odin worship to the island they may have found the ravens already established there as they were in northern Europe. Or they may, as Floki did a thousand years ago, have carried them to Iceland as navagational aids.

Now, economically valueless except as scavengers, they have fallen from their past glory, and are even called the "vultures of the north" for in these degenerate days there are no Vikings to provide the giant black winged birds with well furnished battlefields, and they have to subsist on the carcasses of sheep and other carrion. They still nest in the high crags among the icy glaciers, immune to the inroads of civilization. And as we pass along the plains in a modern bus, out from the untamable timeless mountains may float on blue-black wings a pair of Odin's sacred birds, scouting the approaching enemy as they did so many thousand years ago on the shores of the far-off Danube.

There are seals, too, and in the old days before ships and hunters increased in number they were very plentiful. The gray seal, the harbor seal and the common seal, brown-eyed and sleek, used to follow the salmon up the rivers, leaping and barking, and trail behind a passing boat, attracted by the lights and the sound of music. But nets and harpoons have almost wiped them out. Whales too have almost disappeared, though a few smaller ones are sometimes caught, and what was once an important industry is now confined to the harbor at Hvalfjordur on the west coast. At one time whales were often washed ashore, and the farmers whose homes bordered the harbors used to quarrel so fiercely over the ownership of the stranded animals that they were finally forced to apportion the beaches; now a whale found on one spot may not be claimed by someone further along the strand.

Icelanders today are fond of animals, they treat their dogs well, their horses and cattle are sleek and well cared for, and there are no captive creatures held in zoos. Once a year it is permitted to kill the reindeer, the first herd of which came from Norway in 1771. For the rest of the year they roam, in small numbers, wild and unmolested in the far northwest. They have never been used, as in Lapland, to pull sleds, nor have they been domesticated, herded, or privately owned.

Iceland, then, is the home of birds rather than beasts, with only the fox, a few reindeer, and an occasional polar bear drifting down on ice-floes, to balance against the once famous falcon, the memory of the Great Auk, the profitable eider duck, and other sea-birds which still provide meat and eggs. After more than a thousand years farming is still in its infancy, because of the handicap of the long sterile winter. Farmland is largely unimproved and sheep-ranges unfenced.

Fortunately for the national economy, the Icelander has another source of food and trade. His streams, fjords and the adjacent sea have for centuries been the richest fishing-grounds in the world. Of the three kind of natural fauna, fish, flesh and fowl, it is to the first that the Icelander has long owed his survival. He catches fish, he eats fish, he cures fish, and he may be said to build his houses of fish, since it is the export of fish which pays for the imported wood, iron and cement.

10

Singers and Their Songs

It is often said that Iceland's is the oldest living literature. That word "living" is an important qualification. The Romans were writing, everything from humorous verse to soldiers' war biographies, long before Iceland was known. The *Iliad* and the *Odyssey* are far older, and the Bible makes even these seem like last week's magazine. Nobody knows the age of the ancient Hindu literature, and guesses vary by a thousand years or so.

The point is that these are not "living" literature. The Bible as we know it is a translation. Scholars may read Latin, classical Greek and Sanscrit. But no nations now living still use these ancient tongues. They are dead languages.

Iceland's literature dates back some nine hundred years. The unique and important fact is that present-day Icelanders can still read and understand these 900-year-old tales, in their ancient tongue. Due to their long isolation the Icelanders still speak something very close to the Norse of a thousand years ago. It is as though we still spoke, not the fairly recent speech of Shakespeare, nor even that of Chaucer, but of *Beowulf* and the Anglo-Saxon Chronicles. This is what makes the sagas a truly living literature.

The early tellers of these tales were called skalds. The art of the skald came from Norway, where it dates back to the sixth century, or even earlier. *Beowulf*, in the seventh century Scandinavian chronicles, is of this type of verbal entertainment. Later, skald-craft died out of Norway, but from the tenth century it was preserved in Iceland, and through the following four hundred years became polished and carried to a pitch of perfection never attained elsewhere. By the thirteenth century skald-craft was wholly Icelandic, and so great had it grown that Icelandic skalds were welcomed and honored in the courts throughout Europe.

These men, with their prodigiously trained memories, passed on their complicated art from one generation to the next, the art of the saga-teller, as well as of skaldic poetry. The erudite skaldic poetry died out, but the popular story telling lasted well into the nineteenth century. It was, for a time almost the only possession of the Icelanders, precious both because it was characteristically their own, and because it glorified their magnificent past.

The early skalds chanted their poems to amuse the small royal courts of Norway. Poetry, as we know, is easier to memorize than prose, so these professional entertainers used a kind of unrhymed verse.

The first discovered traces of this skald-craft were already extremely elaborate and intricate in form, far more complicated than any poetry written today. It is quite untranslatable, with its rigid laws of construction. Only scholars of the old Icelandic can take pleasure in its anagrams, doublecrostics, and fantastic embroideries and elaborations. There was also a trick called "kenning"; Alexander Pope used it, but in a simpler form. You mustn't call a spade a spade, it was unpoetical. A simple thing like honey could become "the aureate riches of the Amazonian horde." But skald-craft took it further; "aureate," "Amazonian," and "horde" all had to be altered still further. To translators the meaning is so remote that though every word and sentence is known, the intention of the skald may be utterly lost.

Primitive diplomats and trade emissaries, traveling as far as Constantinople, Rome, Jerusalem and of course, to all the northern courts and kings, and even into what is now called Russia had to be good poets and saga-tellers, as well as good politicians; if they couldn't amuse and interest socially, they were given no chance to plug their goods or put over their message.

Interwoven with the skald craft, and lasting far longer, were the saga and the saga-teller. Saga simply means "something told." So that any recited story was a saga. These varied enormously. Some were short-shorts, mere anecdotes; some were long biographical tales, strictly adhering to the truth; some were mythical, with dragons and magic swords, and mighty deeds of sorcery. There were few love tales, and no fiction as we now know it. The saga teller did not say, "Now I will make up a tale." He carried on from what he had heard from other saga-tellers. Often his tales told to kings related back to them their own exploits in story form, and these had to be strictly based on fact, since the king and all his courtiers knew the truth of what had happened.

There is a tale told of an Icelander coming one summer to the court in Norway, and of being received by the king on condition that he would relate sagas as long as he was required. This he did for many weeks, till, as Christmas time approached, he showed signs of flagging. Was it true, asked the king, that his sagas were giving out? No, but only one saga remained, and that he wished to save for the holy festival.

Then for twelve days this great skald entertained the court with his story telling. And at the end the king asked him how he had remembered so much, and where he had learned the tale. "It is my custom," said the skald, "to go every summer to the Thing, and each summer I learned part of the saga from the great Halldor Snorrason."

Economics affect art. Skald-craft came to a dead end because there were no longer exports to be traded, nor vessels in which to send the goods and the post-envoys. But the saga teller still persisted within the borders of Iceland. Travelers, beggars, occasionally sang for their supper when they stopped at a farm. But no longer in verse.

The sagas of Iceland met much the same need as the Bible in early New England, except that the tales were told of the early champions of their own race, and not of the Israelites, and were not considered inspired. The father or grandfather of the family was the standby, as his stock of tales was likely to be greater than that of younger men, but on occasion the family fund of historical fables would be enriched by a visiting relative, or a nearly professional saga-teller, whose memory might be sharpened by hunger.

The sagas meant a great deal to the Icelanders, although they contained no religious instruction. Their country lost touch with the outer world. Because they did no ploughing, but were graziers, Icelandic farms were larger, their neighbors more distant than in New England. Being further north they had longer nights to get through. They had much smaller houses in which the whole family might be jammed together in one room to get on each others nerves. Finally, for lack of wood, there was no manual occupation such as whittling shoe-pegs, carving wooden bowls, fashioning hay-rakes as men and boys driven in by darkness, sat fidgeting beside the small peat-fire. Picture a day in midwinter, when darkness covered the land for the whole twenty-four hours, babies crying, children quarreling, and men and women lowering at each other, all in one dimly lighted room, and we begin to see the need for a saga-teller, and the tremendous influence of the sagas.

"This is the story of Njal, who was burned in his house by his enemies," the voice would begin. And the peat walls of the hut would lift like a stage-curtain on a land of sunlight, of violence and courage, of noble women, of chieftains dressed in the gold and silver and brightly colored cloth looted from all Europe. Of daring voyages, of shipwrecks, and day-long feasting.

The adult listeners would feel less grim and thwarted as they saw themselves taking part in these great events of their own ancestors, children would stop quarreling, and in the end the steady rumble of the saga-teller's voice would lull even the baby to sleep and silence.

This collection of sagas, both historical and mythical, biographies and accounts of how people live in the past, has been of considerable value to the other northern countries. At the time of the Reformation many libraries and monasteries were looted and burned, civil wars and the downfall of dynasties also took their toll in Europe and in the British Isles. Only Iceland preserved most of her records. Of course, some of these, written on parchment, got lost as well. But so much was preserved, either in direct account, or by inference, of the early history of Europe, that historians have gone to Iceland to fill in the gaps in their knowledge.

The preservation of the Icelandic sagas, and of historical data was begun by a priest, Ari Thorgilsson, known as Ari the Wise. He was born in 1067, and about the year 1120 he began to record the earlier history of his country in his *Islendinga-bok*, where he also gave a short history of the mother-country, Norway. This book was lost long ago, but much of it still exists in abbreviated form, in quotations in other books. Ari was a careful and conscientious scholar, who strove to discriminate between truth and fiction.

Following Ari the Wise came Snorri Sturluson. Born in 1178, he came of a long line of Icelandic chiefs, of skalds, and saga-tellers on both sides of the family, and grew up to be a law-sayer, that is a lawyer. He early began to collect the sagas, also to compose his own poems, one of which he sent to Earl Hacon of Norway. Later he traveled to Norway to try to trace more of the old tales, and to begin his collection called *Heimskringla*. This is a collection of the lives of the Norse Kings, though in the Ynglinga Saga it goes well back into the legends and myths.

Snorre himself lived in the fringes of the bloody Viking era, his own story would be a saga in itself, and he was eventually murdered by order of the Norwegian king, in his own cellar. To read his re-counted sagas is to hear still the clash of arms on steel brynies, the shouts of the invaders, the rattle of oars in rowlocks, and the whir of ravens' wings in the chill lusty air of the north country. They are tales of constant feuds, revenges and counter revenges.

The most famous of these tales of ancient days is the long *Njal's Saga*. Its hero, Burnt Njal, whose nickname was bestowed on him posthumously, was also a law man, or lawyer, and the story tells of the troubles that Njal's sons brought upon themselves and their father. In the end, their numerous enemies, headed by Flosi, surprised and burned them all in their hall. This was in the year 1011. Njal's son-in-law, Kari, succeeded in escaping; the last third of the saga is concerned with the steps taken by him and his friends to avenge the death of their kinsfolk. The characters all come alive and stride through the pages as real and as motivated as though we had known them personally. The burning of Njal's house is one of the great dramatic accounts of all literature.

In the *Saga of Gisli*, a tale of about the same period, the Norse Gisli wrongfully acquires an enchanted sword which is laden with ill fortune. To avenge the honor of his family he commits a series of murders, and voyages from Norway to Iceland. The tale that follows is involved, and again filled with avengings and revenges. In the end the hero is outlawed and killed. All the saga characters seem to end tragically. And, of course, as far as that magic sword is concerned, everyone believed in magic, in good and ill fortune, in incantations and witches, so that magic mixed with history in nowise diminished the historical truth of the saga.

During the dark centuries of near starvation, isolation from Europe and volcanic disasters, it was the sagas and their influence on Iceland and Icelandic education that more than any one other thing served to keep the soul of Iceland alive.

Up to the nineteenth century Iceland had only one public elementary school in the whole country. Before that time the early education of the child was considered largely the responsibility of church and home.

The first schools, founded in the eleventh and twelfth centuries were, as in Europe, largely religious foundations. Then for some two hundred years all teaching declined, and it was not until the fifteenth century that it began to revive again. Yet all during these centuries the sagas, and the *Jonsbook*, the book of Althing laws, were used as textbooks in the home, and it was in the home that instruction was given, with additional teaching of Latin and Danish by local clergymen. During the catholic period there were several Cathedral schools for training of teachers. After 1870 more schools were created, and today there are over two hundred such institutions. All schooling is free, and all children between the ages of seven and sixteen must now attend school. Iceland has no illiteracy.

Country schools are held at the larger farmsteads, the children boarding in one farmstead or another in troops. They study in one farm site for thirteen weeks, then with their teacher move on to another of the widely separated farms. In addition educational radio broadcasts are offered to isolated areas throughout the year.

The beautiful university, on the outskirts of Reykjavik and modeled after European institutions was built in 1940. It was financed by a State lottery, and will eventually include dormitories, laboratories, a gymnasium, etc., as well as the main academic building.

Icelanders are prodigious readers. This is a natural outgrowth of their love of history and of stories, fostered for so many centuries by the sagas. Even the smallest hamlet has its bookstore, filled not with drugstore literature, pulps and comics, but with books of high standard, well bound, even beautifully so, including reference, travel, children's books, and scientific volumes. Iceland reads more books per capita than any other country.

Today Iceland literature is still a living force; the people still cling to their own ancient language, striving to keep it clear of outside influence. It is easy to see why the language of the sagas means so much to the country and its people. Through the long centuries of isolation and hardship, of famine, plagues and destruction by earth-quake and volcano, their courage fed upon the only source available; the sagas.

For this reason the sagas, and the language in which they were told, have, to the Icelanders, become the very soul of Iceland.

11

Folk and Folkways

IT WAS NATURAL that the people of Iceland should develop a strongly marked natural character. All during the Middle Ages they were cut off from any but the rarest contact with Europe. Their literature and language were uninfluenced by interchange with other countries. Their customs, their dress, their habits and even their austere festivities remained purely Icelandic. They had brought from Norway certain basic folkways and these they retained, modified only to suit the difference in climate, the single-crop farming based on sheep, and the lack of wood with which to create new forms in anything from household utensils to architecture.

The first phase of life on the island must have been the same as in Norway, from which the settlers brought both their customs and their lumber for house-building. Everything revolved around the local chieftain and his dwelling place, the "timberhall." Later both timber to build the halls, and thralls to work the land, grew scarce, peasant crofts or small-holdings replaced the chieftains' estates, and sod houses the ancient halls. None of the early Viking-type houses have been preserved, though east of Reykjavik can be seen the recently discovered foundation of what is believed to have been the house of Burnt Njal of the saga of that name.

Here in the great timberhall the women worked all day, for in early Iceland only slaves and a few freemen were farm laborers.

Spinning and weaving was much as it was in our own colonial days. Iceland tweed, woven of the long stapled wool, was much valued for trade. It was called *vadmal*, and was of such quality it was accepted as a standard; six ells of this, about ten yards, counting as the equivalent of one mark in silver, or eight legal ounces. This measure of cloth was for several hundred years commonly used for reckoning values throughout all Scandinavia.

In summer as the women spun, wove, and of course cooked, warriors of the chieftain's bodyguard, called huscarls, lounged or played chess. They also kept in training for the next Viking voyage, the next raid upon a neighbor, or the next raid of a neighbor upon them, by wrestling, running, swimming and contests with spear, bow, ax and sword. Serfs, called thralls, both men and women captured in raids, guarded the grazing sheep and ponies, caught fish on hook or in trap, and cultivated a little, a very little, land.

For several generations this farm life scarcely differed from life in old Norway. Both lands had long dark winters; the Vikings in their own country were accustomed to such grim seasons. Ships went back and forth in summertime very freely, and for a century or more there would have been little difference in luxuries between the two countries. But it is doubtful if the feasting, fighting Norseman who brought with him his own carls and thralls, or who could go out and raid and enslave more household and farm help whenever he wanted to, could forsee the trouble ahead. In old Norway the serfs, thralls, did the farming; the huscarl defended him; and the master of them all, who belonged to the warrior class, scorned the lowly unexciting tasks of agriculture. Where he didn't, and really liked to till the soil and tend his cattle he was given a contemptuous nickname, such as The Farmer.

With the gradual abandonment of Viking raids the chiefs fell into what we now term technological unemployment. Freemen might still indulge in bloody fights, but a professional warrior class was an unproductive business. And with the abandonment of these raids the Icelanders not only lost material imports, which they could exchange for timber and food and other requirements that were produced in more abundance elsewhere, they also found themselves unable to replace dead and worn-out serfs. We can't guess what was the average life of a serf, but we do know that his existence was a hard one in any country, at that period; that he could be slain by his master without penalty, and that if he were killed by another freeman, the freeman paid a fine and forgot the whole business.

So the wastage and deterioration of this human farm implement must have been rapid. And he was no longer replacable by a new model seized off the Scots Islands or the Irish coast. The warriors had to go to work for themselves, and privileges were scarce.

Living conditions in Iceland during the Middle Ages became very bad indeed. Viking ships and Viking halls had moldered away. The house was little more than a turf hut, two or more rooms opening into each other, with a single outside entrance, which helped hold in the heat. The outside walls, of turf or sod fitted between roughly piled stones, were very thick, and the turf roof, supported on thin branches of birch or willow, must have been precarious when sodden with snow or rain. The house from outside was scarcely distinguishable from the earth itself, so tightly did the green roof tie it to the surrounding land. A story is told of a stranger who, urging on his reluctant horse, suddenly crashed down into his host's living room. Through the roof.

Following the turf cottages and predating the modern concrete farmhouse came another kind. This evolved from the turf hut, and though it had no elegance and was crowded, it was far more comfortable than the average farmer's cottage of England a century ago.

Sheep grazing takes vast stretches of land, compared with arable farming, so the houses are widely scattered. Since the hillside pastures remain unchanged through the centuries, present homesteads stand where their predecessors stood, serve the same functions and, until very recently, look much as they must always have looked.

The gabled house in its later development stood alone and lonely in a great sea of grass, with only a few sheds, and scarcely humped above the surrounding meadow; without trees, almost without a garden. Three gables made of the precious wood faced the front. In one of these a tiny entry opened into the general living room. Here the farm laborers slept and ate their meals; the beds and seats were the bunks, there was no dining table. At the head of each bunk a small shelf held the possessions of the occupant, as well as his carved wood food bowl. Into this was poured each morning the food, stew, porridge, skyr, for the day. The carving and decorating of these food bowls, with their wooden hinged cover, was often a winter's occupation for a man as he huddled here for warmth. The women spun, or wove. And, of course, everyone listened to the sagas.

The gable house was two rooms deep. The back room was kitchen, one side piled neatly with stacks of peat. On the crude stone stove, not unlike a campfire barbecue, stood a big iron kettle or two; here too was the bake oven, and a nearby cask held the winter's supply of skyr, clabbered milk.

You clambered to the low second story by a steep ladder or stairway. These two rooms belonged to the farmer's own family, and gave them some degrees of privacy. The beds were narrow bunks, built against the steep sloping walls, the headpiece of one being the footpiece of the next, and everyone bunked in together so that grandmother's feet might rest almost on the head of young Jensson or Jensdotter. But the rooms were cozy, warm with the heat rising from downstairs, and a small glass window in each gable gave light whenever the sun had risen.

These houses were built on a low stone foundation, the crevices plugged with moss and turf. Turf walls, often many feet thick, held out the cold and rain, and small rough stone hallways through which one must crouch gave passage from one gabled room to the next.

The roofs were also of turf, upheld by small birch branches. It was the roof that dictated the gabled architecture, and the lack of logs to make stronger, longer beams that dictated the width of the roof. The length of even a drift wood log was limited by what a pony could carry.

As the farmer grew more prosperous he added more gables to the front of his house; more rooms, all facing the same way, to his original two or three. Another would be workshop, or a cowstall, or a small pen for young lambs. The houses, though crowded, were not uncomfortable and were quite on a level with farm cottages in England at the same period, and far superior to French or Italian housing among workmen.

Naturally these houses did not survive, there is none now existing that is more than a hundred or a hundred and fifty years old. You can see such an old house now used as a museum, a few miles outside of Reykjavik. It belonged to a prosperous fisherman, who also kept sheep; the floors are of wood, there is a small iron stove in every room, and much of the woodwork has been decorated with carving. It was undoubtedly comfortable, and has far more charm, though perhaps not the conveniences of the modern, concrete, state-sponsored structures now being run up all over the country.

Lighting these old houses was as much a problem as heating them. Up to about 1860 horse tallow or whale oil was used in small brass lamps, the wick being of the fluffy cotton grass that one sees in every meadow. Sheep tallow candles, so extensively used in early New England homes seemed to have been used sparingly, if at all, which is odd, because sheep tallow must have been easily procurable.

Today many of the larger farms have their own small lighting plants, run from some nearby waterfall, and power from various stations throughout the island is used in all the towns.

You can still see, on the farms and in the northern country, many women wearing the old national costume. It is pretty, but scarcely flattering, being largely black, lightened only by gold thread lace.

A gold-trimmed black bodice fits tightly over a white blouse with full sleeves; the black skirt is long and full; sometimes a bright-colored or embroidered apron is worn over this, and a belt of filigreed gold or silver, often an heirloom, completes the dress. The headdress is a small round cap with a little turned-back brim like a squashed derby; the hair is worn in two long braids caught up together under this brim, and a long tassel of black silk swings from the peak of the cap; this is confined in the middle by a pipe-like decoration of copper, silver, or ivory. When the wearer wants to be very grand indeed she wears instead a high headdress of sheer lawn over a stiffened support that represents the prow of the Viking ship. The lawn falls in pretty folds about her face, and is charmingly flattering. Few of the young people wear this costume, in fact both boys and girls in their garb could hardly be distinguished from the group on the school bus this morning in any Amercan town. The American soldiers and the movies have done much to spread American fashions wherever they go.

The men, even the older men, no longer wear a distinctive national costume. The Vikings dressed in homespun woolens—we would call them tweeds today. Long cloaks of bright reds and blues, of imported or looted silks and fine wools were caught up on one shoulder with heavy brooches of gold or silver, often of the beautiful Irish gold work. Down through the years the costume altered much as it did in Europe, keeping a slack pace with foreign fashions. Old style working shoes were made of sheepskin, or sealskin, heelless, the heel being replaced by an inside pad of moss. These were practical because they were homemade, but were not very durable. A long foot journey used to be measured in so many shoe lengths, that is how many shoes of the fragile sealskin would be worn out during the journey.

The women of Iceland have always been very independent. And nowhere does this independence show more clearly than in their names. Centuries before the American woman claimed the right to use her own name and not her husbands in business or in the arts, the Icelandic girl retained her own by rights, even within marriage. In fact she never lost that right.

It is still true today, and though at first it seems an odd arrangement, it is quite simple, once the pattern is mastered. She does not take her father's last name, his family name, she takes his first name, and tacks onto it "daughter"—that is *dotter*. So that John Jones' daughter would not be called "Jones," but "Johnsdaughter," or "Jensdotter." John Jones' son would not be "Jones" either, he would be "John's son," or "Jenssen." The girls keep their own names after they are married and in turn their sons and daughters will take on the first name of their mother's husband, their father. This means a change of family name every generation.

But to the outsider this nomenclature is sometimes confusing. For instance if you want to telephone a family. Is the telephone in the name of the husband, or in the name of the wife if she happens also to be in business? Or does the married daughter, living at home, have a phone in her own name? In a family of four, husband, wife, daughter and son, there would be four last names, Jon Magnusson, then his wife, Elizabeth Grimmerdotter, his son Hakon Jonsson, and his daughter, Maria Jonsdotter.

This taking on the father's first name is true not only, as in old Norway, with the eldest son . . . and could be compared to our John Jones Junior . . . but with the second, third and fourth sons. In old Norway only the oldest boy took his father's name, succeeding sons took on, as a family name, the name of their farm or property, much as was done in England. The Vikings, who broke free from any place names when they came to still nameless properties in Iceland, had to retain the father's name.

The nostalgic transplanted Norwegians held family and background to be of considerable importance; this is strongly borne out in the sagas where long lists of genealogies preceed every story—like the "begats" of the Bible . . . and for the same reason. The early Biblical people were nomads, often in strange lands; the Vikings were transplanted. Both felt a pride in their ancestry. Both, perhaps because they owned livestock and depended on them, realized the importance of breeding. Humans were animals, and knowing the stock from which they came allowed you a good clue to what they were worth, as friends or enemies. In those days it could matter a lot.

Our English, French and German names have evolved in several different ways; a man named John might be called by a descriptive nickname, "John the Red" or "John Scarlett." Then there was a name evolved from John's craft; John Fletcher who was "John the maker of arrows"; John Smith who was "John the Blacksmith," or goldsmith. Or there was "John of Nottingham," who became plain "John Nottingham." And finally John who had no other distinction than to be son of his father Robert. Hence he became "John Robertson."

The early Icelanders had no special craft save that of fighting from which to evolve a name. So as a means of identification, they used a nickname. There might be many Leifs in the country, but the one we know was called "Leif the lucky one." There might be many Erics, so the one we know was tagged with the color of his beard, "Eric the Red." There were many Haralds, so we know of "Harald Bluetooth," "Harald Goatbeard," and "Harald Fairhair," who because of a vow let his hair grow long, and who, before he cut it was also tagged with the nickname of "Harald the Lousy" . . . perhaps by his enemies.

It is interesting that one finds few Irish names in Iceland, yet after the Norse chiefs had succeeded so efficiently in killing off each other many of the properties would have descended to their Scottish or Irish freedmen; there is mention of this in the sagas. Did these freed Irish and Scottish slaves immediately adapt Icelandic names? It is probable, for they would have dropped their national Celtic speech and adopted that of the people around them. The Irish genes were strong and it is not difficult even after a thousand years to recognize today the Irish build and facial structure among the islanders, especially among the men.

It is usual for the males of a ruling race to take serf women as wives or concubines. To a lesser extent, for it would be frowned upon, when constant and deadly feuds reduced the number of possible husbands of their own race Norse women may have taken serf husbands. It is also likely that peasant-minded serf families survived the series of cataclysms and famines better than their warrior masters. Strength, skill at arms and courage in battle would have less survival value in such grim times than the peasant ability to make do with little and also take first pick of the scanty crops. Whatever may be the reason, or combination of reasons, the Irish characteristics in Iceland are far more noticeable than one would expect.

Iceland has had in the past few festivities. Neighbors were too far from each other and pony travel was difficult, even dangerous, especially for the women. Half the year was dark, and it was time-wasting to try to get to talk to a neighbor five or ten or twenty miles away. In the old days the gathering at the Thingvellir was the year's greatest feast and picnic. Next to that would be the farmer's sheep shearing, which occurs in July, and the in-folding in the autumn.

Of these two the July shearing was, and still is, the one most welcomed by the young people. For women attend this as well. It occurs in the high mountains and often lasts a week. Here the farmers gather with their wives and their children. The days are busy with gathering the sheep and the shearing, but the nights are active too, and as in midsummer there is little difference in the amount of daylight, dancing may go on till morning; the harmonicas, the accordions and guitars repeat the old songs, and even a few new ones heard on the radio. The older women wear their gold embroidered national costumes, the young ones appear in their brightest sweaters. It is a very gay time indeed.

The in-folding, which starts on St. Matthew's Day, the Sunday nearest September twentieth, is more serious and far less festive.

Only the young boys go with their fathers and grandfathers—it is a sign that they have reached manhood when they are taken along, and farm boys who have gone to work in town often return home for this task. Already it is early dark and the high curtains of the Northern Lights illumine the skies, as the shouting, laughing groups start out from the farm houses.

As the highest ranges are reached, each mounted man and boy takes up his station, the tough little sheep dogs know their job. Circling the small flocks that follow each great ram they herd them slowly into the ever-growing bands.

Sometimes it is misty, or the rain pelts down. Then the work is difficult and dangerous. But at last the great bands reach the community pens, where the sheep are counted and apportioned out, each bleating, blatting, struggling herd to its own farmer. These go into the winter fields, nearer the home farm, for the hills will soon be snowed in. The work done, a big feast is spread. This may be the last time for many weeks when neighbors can get together and exchange news and gossip, before the young people return to their town jobs and the hard work of the winter farm begins.

In what is a remarkably mild climate compared with Scandinavia, Canada, and the northern part of the United States, it is the length and the darkness of winter which is the greatest handicap to farmers, not its severity. Sheep and to a lesser extent ponies may fend for themselves in the lower meadows which have been reserved for their winter grazing, but dairy stock must be stall-fed for half the year.

Since there is almost no tillage, there is no silage or grain for feed, and hay becomes of supreme importance. Fortunately the little there is is said to be unusually nutritious. It looks more like overgrown lawn than meadow grass, dense, but barely long enough to cut with a scythe. In fact much of the hay does come from lawns, from the university campus to little patches in city gardens, some so small that one would expect them to be hayed with scissors and table-fork. In a land with what seems to a stranger rather grandiose ideas for the future, this careful husbandry of resources is reassuring.

If ever a country cultivated a split personality it is Iceland. With all her might she intends to cling to her old ways, especially culturally. Her sagas are still considered her greatest literature; as they should be, of course. But she also clings to the language of the sagas, sternly vowing that no harsh echo of the modern world shall corrupt her long-cherished Icelandic speech.

On the other hand, in all technical matters and in commerce and the adoption of modern gadgets, she is racing to catch up with the rest of the world. This means running very fast indeed, because for so many hundreds of years she lived far out on the perimeter of the commercial world, untouched, almost uninfluenced by it.

In her most important industry, fishing, Iceland has been quick to take on everything modern she could lay hands to. Radar, sonar, radio, ship-to-shore telephone, meteorology and all its scientific equipment have been called on to aid this oldest of Iceland's crafts, and the one by which she may yet survive or perish. She is in stiff competition with England, with our own fishing fleets, with Portugal and Spain for the fish markets of the world. She cannot afford to slip backwards here, into the days of the sagas.

The efficiency of farming methods is difficult to assess. Wheeled and caterpillar tractors and bulldozers, mostly left over from the American occupation, can be seen on almost every lowland farm. They seem at first sight a costly luxury, as are the spacious reinforced concrete farmhouses subsidized by government. Where almost no ploughing is done, and the farmer's mainstay is sheep grazing on unimproved and scarcely improvable mountain ranges, the maintenance of so much machinery seems rather a burden than an asset.

But once long ago Iceland grew a little grain. It must have been a risky luxury crop. In the hand-to-mouth living of successive centuries this crop was abandoned. But important, though small-scale, experiments are being made to find a grain which can mature in the short northern summer. If it is found, the tractors may become invaluable, supplying home-grown grain instead of costly imported flour for the nation's bread, and silage of some sort to allow more dairy cattle to supply more milk.

Everywhere the Icelanders are up against crippling handicaps. Livestock could be doubled and trebled at once, but for the scarcity of winter fodder. Forestry can make little progress for lack of fence posts to protect young plantations. The urgent need for progress along every technical line is limited by lack of mechanics and crafts-men of every kind. This appalling handicap stretches all the way from politicians with no big-business training, who are confronted with the incredibly difficult task of organizing a whole nation as an intricate welfare state, to the problem of the humble honeybee. The people have no home-grown honey to reduce the importation of sugar, because it is said there is not enough nectar for the bees to gather. There is not enough nectar because there are no bees to pollinate and spread the existing thyme, clover and heather upon the eroding hillsides. So erosion increases and there is no honey.

Due to the need to import almost all the necessities of modern life from flour to hydroelectric plants, the Icelanders are living far beyond their means. They are said to have the highest debt, per head, of any country in the world. It is imperative that they become more self-supporting. Yet even a stranger can see on every side the chains of the past which bind them.

The country is making gallant and almost desperate efforts to break out from these chains which fetter it to its past, while still retaining what seems to an observer the highest popular standard of culture in the world.

And Iceland seems to be unique in its firm resolve not to sacrifice its spiritual values and cultural legacy to material progress. It intends to have both!

INDEX

Akureyri, 13, 83-84
Althing, 22-27, 32, 36, 66
America, discovery by Leif, 57-62
Animals, 96-104; cattle, 98; dog, 99-100;
  fox, 99; horse, 97; sheep, 98; whale, 103
Artists, 75

Beasts, see animals
Bifrost, 77-79
Biarne, discovers America, 56
Birds, 82, 96, 98-99, 100-104; eider duck,
  102; falcon, 100-101; great auk, 101-102;
  raven, 102-103; water birds, 101
Brattalid (on Greenland), 43, 49, 57

Canadian and British troops, 36
Christianity, comes to Iceland, 27
Climate, 9; and weather, 15, 68
Columbus, Christopher, 55
Constitution granted, 35
Co-operatives, 83

Denmark, 31-32, 33, 35-36; expedition to
  Greenland, 50; and Greenland, 52-53
Dettifoss, 13
Dog, Iceland, see animals

Earthquakes, 13, 32, 66
Eric the Red, 41, 53, 57
Eskimos, in Greenland, 44-45, 50, 52, 53

Farms, and farming, 81, 123
Farm animals, see animals
Faxafloi, 64
Fish, and fishing, 70-72, 104, 123
Flag, Icelandic, 101
Floki, 18

Food, 79-80
Forestry, 84
Freydis, sister to Leif, 61

Gardar, discoverer of Iceland, 19
Geology, 9
Geysir, Great, 12, 15
Glaciers, 15, 85
Godafoss, 13
Greenland, 22, 41-54, 56, 58
Gullfoss, 14
Gulf Stream, 15

Hafnarfjondur, fishing village, 70
Hallormsstadur, forestry, 84, 92-93
Harald Fairhair, 19, 119
Hekla, 10-11
Herjolfness, 50, 52
Houses, 115, 117, see also Reykjavik
  chapter

Indians, 59
Industries, 72
Irish, 20, 72, 120

Jonsson, Einars, artist, 75

Karlsefni, Thorfinn, 55, 59-62
Keflavik, 38

Language, 95, 123
Leif the Lucky, 46, 55, 57; statue of, 75
Literature, see Sagas
Location, of Iceland, 9

Magnusson, Skuli, 35
Mount Desert (U.S.A.), 58

125

Museum, 74
Myvatn Lake, 82-83

Nomenclature, 118
Norway, 65, 107, 113
Norway and Norsemen, 20-21; Norway and Greenland, 48, 52
Norway, treaty with, 30

Olafsson, Eggert, 35
Oxara, 22-23

Petursson, Hallgrimur, and the Passion Hymns, 34

Reykjavik, 13, 63-76; old houses in, 113; first settled, 19, 35

Sagas and Eddas, 27, 33, 56, 105-112
Schools, 111
Seamen, home for aged, 73
Sheep, shearing, 121; raising, 93-94
Sigurdsson, Jon, 35

Skalds and skald singers, 105
Snorre, first white child born in America, 55, 60, 62
Sturluson, Snorri, 109-110

Theatre, National, 66
Thingvellir, 36
Thorgeir, 27
Thorgilsson, Ari (Ari the Wise), 109
Thorvald, Leif's brother, 58

Ulfgot, 22
United Nations and NATO, 39
U.S.A., 38; and Greenland, 53, 118

Vatnajokull, 11
Vikings, 13, 21, 23, 24, 42-48, 53, 74, 97, 114, 118
Viking age, death of, 49
Vinland, *see* America
Volcanoes, 11, 12, 32

Westman, Islands, 10, 20

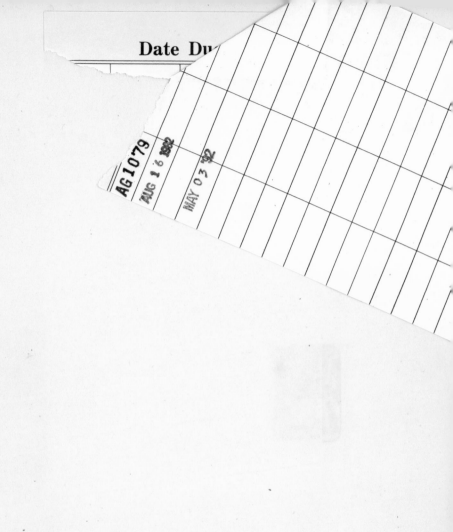